Mark Antony Shead was born in 1990 in the London Borough of Bexley, where he has lived much of his life to date. He graduated from the University of East Anglia in 2012 in modern history, before starting his career as an account manager in Japanese reinsurance business at Aon.

With thanks for the support of my Aon colleagues, friends and family, and special thanks to Jerad for the chat over a few beers in Canada that made this book happen.

Mark Antony Shead

SCRAMBLE FOR CROWNS

The Fascinating Stories of Europe's
Modern Royals

AUSTIN MACAULEY PUBLISHERS™

LONDON * CAMBRIDGE * NEW YORK * SHARJAH

A CIP catalogue record for this title is available from the British Library.

ISBN 9781528990905 (Paperback)
ISBN 9781528990912 (ePub e-book)

www.austinmacauley.com

First Published (2021)
Austin Macauley Publishers Ltd
25 Canada Square
Canary Wharf
London
E14 5LQ

Preface

One of the much-cited assets of the institution of monarchy is that it is associated with continuity, which in turn is associated with stability. And on the face of it, you can see why. With a republic, it is difficult to predict who the head of state will be in five to ten years, let alone twenty to fifty years. But with a monarchy, it should be a very different story. After all, when a Briton looks at a photograph of their royal family today, one that includes Queen Elizabeth II and princes Charles, William and George, it would not be unreasonable for that Briton to expect to be looking upon their present and future national leaders for the rest of their lives. But, if modern history is anything to go by, no European can take the institution of monarchy for granted. Just over one hundred years ago (increasingly the length of an average human lifespan), an overwhelming majority of Europeans had a royal as their head of state. And yet, today, Europe's reigning kings and queens, princes and grand dukes are now clearly in a minority, as their numbers have been whittled down for a variety of reasons, whether brought down by the barricades of revolution, the bayonets of war or the ballot boxes of modern democracy. Thus, if we look at the experiences of Europe's modern royals as a whole, whilst we can sometimes see an orderly succession, in recent times there has also clearly been a scramble for crowns, a scramble to take or to keep the thrones of Europe, with mixed results.

This book recounts the fascinating stories of twenty-six royals from across Europe who have shaped, and been shaped, by the modern era. Although each chapter focuses on an individual, all of their stories are in some way interwoven and overlap and, collectively, they outline the experiences of royal houses, of countries, and of Europe generally. Moreover, the extensive intermarriages between European royals and dynasties over the generations expand the relationships we are about to see from normal international relations to family ties as well. Monarchy's reliance on the accident of birth rather than elections also ironically means that, despite the narrow gene pool, in some ways we get the opportunity to see a greater range of people than is generally the case with politicians: more of a balance between leaders who are male and female, old and young, good and bad, wise and foolish.

Monarchy's heyday appears to have passed, but royals still reign in 10 European countries (12 if you include non-hereditary monarchies as well) and, as you will see, just because a monarchy comes to an end does not mean that the corresponding royal families suddenly disappear without a trace. Of course, to cover every monarch (or head of a royal family) in every European country would be an epic task, and an epic read. That is why, to ease you in, what follows is a selection of stories that combine the drama and variety that modern European monarchy has to offer. The chapters are in a chronological order, based on when the individual concerned either inherited their respective crown or claim to a crown, occurring at any time from the French Revolution of 1789 until the present day. To anticipate potential confusion, when referring to claims to a throne or crown, this means someone who is regarded by their supporters as the monarch of a country that has been reformed into a republic. At the end of this book are the Gallery, which puts faces to the names of those covered by a chapter, and the Appendices: the first providing an overview of the reigning royal houses featured in this book, and the second an illustration of the closest descendants of Queen Victoria of Great Britain, to demonstrate how tightly linked many of Europe's leaders really were.

Napoleon

Only 10 years earlier it would have been impossible to predict not only that, after centuries as a kingdom, France would be reformed as an empire, but that the well-established monarchical principle of hereditary succession would be disregarded to allow a commoner (i.e., someone of non-royal blood), Napoleon Bonaparte, to become its first emperor in 1804. Napoleon proved to be not just any commoner though.

By the end of the early modern era, the Kingdom of France ranked amongst Europe's Great Powers (and was arguably its foremost) which also included the Kingdom of Great Britain (soon to become the United Kingdom of Great Britain and Ireland), the Holy Roman Empire (shortly to be reformed as the Austrian Empire), the Russian Empire, and the Kingdom of Prussia, the latter covering the north of present day Germany and beyond into the east. However, exasperation with France's ruling elite amongst certain elements of French society culminated in the French Revolution of 1789, which brought the early modern age to an end, and marked the beginning of the period often characterised as modernity. Though the Revolution was not initially directed at the monarchy, the attempt by King Louis XVI to flee the country in disguise, out of fear of the Revolution's continued escalation, made the French royal family enemies of the state. Thus, France was declared a republic, while the guillotine, the efficient alternative means of execution whereby a blade was dropped onto the victim's neck within a wooden frame (as opposed to the more haphazard technique of an axe-wielding executioner), was used to end the lives of the King and Queen of France. The number of targets for further executions spread like wildfire, and the guillotine's victims would soon include the revolutionary leaders themselves that had advocated using it in the first place.

The repercussions of the Revolution would soon be felt elsewhere, as European leaders rushed to condemn the execution of King Louis and his wife, Queen Marie Antoinette. This was in solidarity not only with the French monarchs as fellow royals but also as family members; this deeper relationship resulting from the historic interbreeding of European royalty that had been encouraged as a means to securing alliances. Queen Marie Antoinette herself was a classic case of this, as she was born an Austrian Archduchess and therefore a member of the House of Habsburg. Tensions between revolutionary France and royal Europe soon culminated in war. However, war abroad with the combined forces of Europe's other Great Powers, and escalating unrest at home, soon exhausted France and she burnt herself out. Out of France's ultimate defeat in the Revolutionary Wars however emerged a figure who had been repeatedly associated with French victories overseas: Napoleon Bonaparte. The man who had risen through France's military ranks would now do the same in politics until, in 1804, Napoleon had himself duly crowned Emperor of the French.

Emperor Napoleon promptly began his legendary campaign of conquest across Europe, and within the space of a decade managed to dominate the continent. His approach was threefold: direct control and annexation of territory to France; sponsoring puppet states ruled by his family members, for example having his brother Joseph crowned King Jose of Spain; and making peace with existing powerful rulers, notably Tsar Alexander I of Russia and Emperor Francis of Austria. As has been mentioned, Emperor Napoleon was a commoner, and he surrounded himself with those who had achieved success based not on noble heritage but merit. The most significant members of Napoleon's elite were the Marshals of France, appointed to share responsibility with him for managing the Empire and its military campaigns, who included Jean Bernadotte amongst others. In spite of these meritocratic foundations to Napoleonic rule, Emperor Napoleon also embraced aspects of the old royal order, be it through granting himself the monarchical title of emperor (complete with a coronation so elaborate that it was said to have made the future King George IV of Great Britain jealous and want to outdo him), as well as appointing his family members as monarchs across Europe so that the dynasty of the House of Bonaparte could join the ranks of the established Bourbons and Habsburgs. In addition, Emperor Napoleon ditched his wife, Josephine, and married Archduchess Marie-Louise of Austria, with whom he hoped to produce an heir of traditional European royal blood. By marrying into a prestigious European dynasty, Emperor Napoleon could boost his own legitimacy, while his prospective heirs could also be regarded as equals to Europe's established royals.

By sweeping across Europe and toppling many of its rulers, Emperor Napoleon ensured that his legacy would endure around the continent. Removing long-established rulers exposed their vulnerability to the masses, ensuring their fallibility would never be forgotten. He also removed and redrew national borders, which included the dissolution of the centuries-old Holy Roman Empire(promptly reformed into the Austrian Empire). Up and down Central Europe, he would set templates for countries of the future: uniting the numerous states of Northern Central Europe into the Confederation of the Rhine, and doing the same in the southern centre to create the Kingdom of Italy, establishing the precursors for Germany and Italy respectively that would be reformed later in the century. Emperor Napoleon's legal code would inspire those of France and elsewhere but, unsurprisingly, it was within his own country that his legacy would be most enduring. This man who was barely French (Emperor Napoleon was born in Corsica, an island which hitherto had only been under French rule for as long as he'd been alive) would become probably the most famous person from France in history, with all subsequent French leaders left in his shadow.

Despite his continent-wide influence, Emperor Napoleon could not preserve the status quo favourable to him and his new House of Bonaparte indefinitely. Those now living under the Bonaparte dynasty were growing restless, and could count on the enduring support of Emperor Napoleon's relentless foe: Great Britain. Hitherto, Great Britain had experienced repeated knockbacks in the face of the First French Empire, but ongoing British hostility had stirred Emperor Napoleon's anger, manifesting itself in the establishment of the continental system, setup to exclude Great Britain from European trade in an attempt to bring down her economy, and consequently her continual opposition as well. However, his attempts were unsuccessful, and a coalition of European powers, including Great Britain, brought down the Napoleonic Empire. This demise was hastened by Emperor Napoleon's infamous error (repeated in the next century by Adolf Hitler) of invading his former ally, Russia, and falling in the face of not only

Russian determination, but the country's vast and unforgiving landscape and harsh winters. This allowed the army of Tsar Alexander I to push Emperor Napoleon's forces all the way back across the continent to Paris, where the Russian Tsar was able to parade triumphantly through the streets on horseback. Emperor Napoleon's defeat in 1814 led to him being transported, seemingly out of harm's way, to the small Mediterranean island of Elba, where he would have the courtesy title of 'Emperor'. Meanwhile, Europe's Great Powers would attempt to restore the continent's national borders and leaders in Napoleon's wake. They would do so at a grand summit called the Congress of Vienna, hosted by the Austrian Empire, with the wily Emperor Francis of Austria and his sharp-eyed Chancellor, Klemens von Metternich, leading the proceedings.

Before a final settlement could be reached though, Napoleon managed to escape Elba, return to France, and rally supporters to back him in restoring his French Empire. His success would only last 100 days before he was defeated once and for all in the famous Battle of Waterloo by an army led by the British Duke of Wellington. Napoleon would be sent to a more distant exile this time, in St Helena, a remote British-controlled island in the Atlantic Ocean, where he would remain until his death in 1821. News of his death spread, with King George IV of Great Britain amongst those duly informed. This would have been of particular interest to him as he had been Great Britain's Prince Regent, and thereby acting head of state, during the latter part of the Napoleonic Wars, taking on royal duties whilst his father, King George III, descended into madness. King George IV's reaction to Napoleon's death initially may have seemed surprising. To first give some context, King George IV had had an incredibly difficult relationship, virtually since his wedding, with his wife, Queen Caroline, who had repeatedly undermined him during both his Regency and then his early reign as King. And so, when word of Napoleon's death reached Britain, and King George IV was duly informed that "your greatest enemy is dead", he replied, "Is she, by God?"

Karl

In 1818, Karl XIII was succeeded by Karl XIV as King of Sweden. On the face of it, this seems like an uneventful transition from one monarch to the other, with their shared names implying a general commonality between them. However, the first of these monarchs was the son of a Swedish king and counted kings of Denmark and Prussia among his illustrious ancestors; the latter of these monarchs, meanwhile, was born a middle-class Frenchman called Jean Bernadotte.

Born in 1763, Bernadotte would soon embark on a military career that would coincide with that of Napoleon Bonaparte, with both men distinguishing themselves within the French army during the Revolutionary Wars in the wake of the French Revolution. As they rose through the ranks of the French military, the paths of Napoleon and Bernadotte came together and the two developed a mutual respect for each other. Upon becoming Emperor of the French, Napoleon made Bernadotte one of his Marshals of France: high ranking members of Napoleon's imperial elite who would be entrusted to lead military campaigns and oversee newly-acquired territories during the Napoleonic Wars. Bernadotte's fiery temperament yet effective military skill made him a memorable man, but his ability to also be a merciful and respectful captor when it came to prisoners of war would also stand him in good stead in unexpected ways.

Amongst the prisoners of war he would be responsible for during the Napoleonic Wars were high-ranking members of the Swedish army. Bernadotte treated them well and, in turn, they would come to admire Bernadotte's qualities. Meanwhile, back in Sweden, despite being amongst the oldest monarchies in the world, at the time the Swedish throne had been suffering from instability and an unsteady line of succession. During the Napoleonic Wars, Sweden's monarch was King Karl XIII, who by this point was an elderly man and therefore highly unlikely to father any children who could inherit the throne, raising the prospect of yet another succession crisis for the country. In the past, as well as in the future, the usual response of European politicians to such a situation was for the ruling elite to either trace through the family tree until a successor, however distantly related, could be found; or otherwise find a distinguished royal (usually German) who was without a throne to fill the vacancy. In this instance though, influential Swedes were mindful of how, on the one hand, Emperor Napoleon's France was dominating Europe; and on the other, what a hero and respectable man Jean Bernadotte had seemed when they came across him. Appointing one of Napoleon's Marshals as Sweden's king appeared to present a good opportunity for the country to secure a comfortable life for itself within a French-dominated Europe. Moreover, amongst Sweden's national ambitions was to secure control of Norway from Denmark, which might be easier to achieve if the heir to the Swedish throne had the ear of Emperor Napoleon.

And so, in the midst of the Napoleonic Wars, Bernadotte was offered the throne of Sweden, an offer he accepted. Emperor Napoleon was unsure what to make of this development: this meant that one of his key allies would soon be sitting upon the throne of another European country; but then again, when push came to shove, could Bernadotte's loyalties to France always be counted upon to trump those of his adopted country of Sweden? These questions over whether a monarch ultimately owed allegiance to their country of birth or heritage, or the country they newly found themselves leading, would be raised time and again in Europe, as the European nations regularly imported and exported their royals to each other. A century later, greater intensity would be added to these questions as many Europeans found themselves led by German-born royals during a war in which the German Empire was deemed their countries' greatest enemy.

By accepting the offer of the Swedish throne, Bernadotte now played a leading role in Swedish politics and, thanks to his experience, military affairs as well, with the support of Sweden's generals and politicians, and the guidance of the aged King Karl XIII. Over time, Emperor Napoleon's apprehension would become more and more justified, with Napoleonic rule in Europe becoming increasingly unpopular, and Sweden's interests therefore more likely to be served if she were to fight *against,* rather than *alongside,* France. This was not a comfortable situation for Bernadotte, but one that he accepted, with the national interests of Sweden now uppermost in his mind.

By the end of the Napoleonic Wars, the heir to the Swedish throne was a respected figure and war veteran. He was also able to secure union between Norway and Sweden under the Swedish crown, although this was a controversial move for the many Norwegians who had hoped for independence, despite the high regard in which Bernadotte was held. However, the cession of control of Finland from Sweden to the Russian Empire went ahead, as discussed towards the end of the Napoleonic Wars. Then, in a sign of both continuity at his accession and respect for the man who had effectively been an adopted father-figure, Bernadotte chose to take on his predecessor's name and called himself King Karl XIV of Sweden. As King, Karl XIV would at times come to blows with Swedish politicians due to his short temper and conservative views, and would struggle to get his opinions across given that his mother tongue was French and had a limited grasp of the Swedish language. Nevertheless, his silver jubilee in 1843, marking 25 years on the Swedish throne, was widely celebrated, taking place a year before his death.

Upon King Karl XIV's death the succession was a smooth one, with the throne passing to his son, the new King Oscar I, who had spent his adult life being groomed to inherit the Swedish throne. Traditional European royal blood would soon flow through the Swedish royal family's veins once again as King Karl XIV had secured the marriage of his son and successor to Josephine, Duchess of Leuchtenberg. Though Sweden's union with Norway would prove less enduring, it still lasted for almost a century before Norway voted to become an independent kingdom in 1905, and chose a Danish prince to re-establish her own monarchy and become King Haakon VII of Norway. The monarchy continues to this day in both Norway and Sweden, while King Karl XIV's House of Bernadotte retains the Swedish throne.

Louis Philippe

France brought revolution to Europe once again in 1830 and, although the removal of King Charles X of France was followed soon after by the accession of King Louis Philippe, this demonstrated that significant cracks were appearing in the façade of the European order established only 15 years earlier at the Congress of Vienna. Part of the settlement was that Emperor Napoleon would be replaced as France's head of state by King Louis XVIII, brother of the former King Louis XVI who had been guillotined following the 1789 French Revolution. Although no-one had been crowned king between the two King Louis's, King Louis XVIII felt that the uncrowned son and heir of his predecessor, who died in a Paris prison during the course of France's revolutionary republic, should still have been recognised as France's last monarch, an uncrowned King Louis XVII.

King Louis XVIII's coronation marked the restoration of France's traditional House of Bourbon, albeit with some concessions of greater freedom promised to the public in an effort to avoid a revolution from happening again. However, whilst this was something King Louis XVIII was willing to accept, his brother and successor, King Charles X, was not. Over the course of what would be a six-year reign, King Charles X set about gradually eroding those rights and freedoms permitted by his predecessor. This was tolerated for a time but, by 1830, when King Charles X attempted to further bolster his political power, with the ambition to reconstruct France once more as a conservative nation with a powerful monarchy, revolution erupted on the streets of Paris again.

At arm's length from these developments was a famously more liberal branch of the French royal family, the House of Orleans, which had provoked great resentment amongst French royals and their supporters for fighting alongside the revolutionary republican forces which had deposed and executed King Louis XVI. Unsurprisingly, relations remained difficult between the Bourbon monarchs and their Orleanist cousins when King Louis XVIII was made King of France. Interestingly though, this distance and these differences would ultimately come to benefit the head of the House of Orleans, Duke Louis Philippe of Orleans, as the French elite frantically searched for an alternative leader following the ousting of King Charles X. Although King Charles X had put forward his young grandson, Henri, as his nominated successor as a consequence of the revolution, he was not felt to be an acceptable choice. Having said this, given the great instability associated with both republicanism and the Napoleonic Empire over recent decades, these were not considered wise alternatives to the conventional Kingdom of France. France's options therefore seemed to be limited, and there was concern that the country would return to the anarchic state associated with the revolutionary republic, a prospect many within France and elsewhere in Europe feared.

As it was, on the opposite side of Europe, the ancient nation of Greece was fighting for independence from the Islamic Ottoman Empire, a far-reaching country based in present-day Turkey. The Greek cause attracted the sympathies of many Europeans, including from those leaders who generally feared change, and were concerned with the stability of Europe and the order they had established at the Congress of Vienna. Moreover, later in 1830 other uprisings were inspired by the events in France, with the Catholic Belgians fighting to break free from the Protestant United Kingdom of the Netherlands, and the Polish were hoping to form an independent country once more after their country had been dismembered by Prussia, Austria and Russia towards the end of the eighteenth century.

To the relief of many at home and abroad during these changeable times, Louis Philippe would emerge out of the 1830 revolution as the epitome of compromise for France: while acceptable to conservative public feeling as a member of the French royal family, he was also a royal that would be far more willing to embrace the changes brought to France and its people since the revolution than the more conservative Bourbon dynasty. Louis Philippe was therefore crowned King, and from the outset showed off his liberal principles: when accepting the throne, he did so in full public view wrapped in the tricolour flag, the flag of both the First French Republic and Napoleon's Empire. He also called himself King of the French, not King of France, in a display of effort to connect more with his people than the country generally.

Throughout his life until then, whether literally fighting to uphold the changes brought about by the French republic, or during his exile in Great Britain, the new King Louis Philippe had immersed himself in liberal values and ideas. As monarch, King Louis Philippe then pledged to oversee a liberal regime that would protect those rights and freedoms that had been undermined by the Bourbons. King Louis Philippe intended to model his leadership of France on the constitutional monarchy he had experienced during his exile in Great Britain, i.e., a governmental system whereby the monarch had powers reserved, and could generally oversee the governance of the country, but in practice power would ultimately rest with an elected government and parliament.

Within and outside of France, there was general optimism among politicians and royalty that prolonged revolution and instability had been averted, and that King Louise Philippe's liberal kingdom could be a sustainable model. Given King Louis Philippe's ties and sympathies with Great Britain, many in that country saw the arrival of this new French monarch as an opportunity for a fresh start for what had historically been frosty relations between Britain and France. However, just as British politicians were putting plans in place to rejuvenate Anglo-French relations, Great Britain's new (not to mention misshapen) monarch, King William IV, made an unhelpful intervention: he decided that this would be an appropriate time to make a public speech in which he would conclude that, whether at war or at peace, France would always be Great Britain's natural enemy. When a journalist then questioned a politician about the King's speech, the exasperated politician responded with regards to his monarch: "What can you expect from a man with a head like a pineapple?" Nevertheless, following King William IV's death, those looking forward to warmer ties between France and Great Britain had their wish come true, as one of the most cordial royal relationships enjoyed between the two countries was established between King Louis Philippe and Great Britain's young Queen Victoria. This was demonstrated by the decision of the two monarchs to invite each other on state visits to their respective countries, the first time this had occurred for centuries. Aside from the friendly personal connection between these nations' royals, this new relationship would have a broader impact on international relations. Great Britain, and now France as well under King Louis Philippe, would be Europe's great defenders of liberalism; encouraging democracy and supporting the rights of new nations across the continent, in opposition to the conservative Great Power alliance of Austria, Russia and Prussia.

For all of King Louis Philippe's championing of liberal values and democracy at home and abroad though, in practice it is usually the economy and people's standard of living that shapes public opinion. And, unfortunately for King Louis Philippe, the French economy continued to be fragile during his reign and the public were growing tired of seeing little change in their quality of life. Moreover, the King himself attracted mockery: just as the British King William IV was ridiculed for looking like a pineapple, in later life King Louis Philippe would be unfavourably compared with a pear in the press. By 1848, it appeared that the Paris mob had had enough of their elderly, pear-shaped monarch, prompting protests on the street. When the demonstrators were met by King Louis Philippe's soldiers, shots were fired and the situation escalated. While, in response, King Louis Philippe dismissed his prime minister, the influential Francois Guizot, this was not yet enough to deter demonstrators from erecting barricades: the tell-tale sign of yet another revolution in France. King Louis Philippe therefore abdicated (i.e., gave up his right to the throne), and in response it was decided that France should have a second stab at a republic. Meanwhile, this revolution in France inspired extensive unrest across Europe, with the 1848 revolutions having a broader and more significant impact on the continent than the relatively limited uprisings of 1830. Meanwhile, Louis Philippe would spend the few remaining years of his life in Great Britain, where he was exiled to once again.

Otto

Germany has long been renowned as a great exporter. However, whilst nowadays German exports tend to be associated with Volkswagens and BMWs, in the nineteenth century Germans were more renowned for exporting their royals. One such case of this was in 1832, when Greece received Prince Otto of Bavaria, son of King Ludwig I of Bavaria, by way of a British warship, and accepted him as King Otto of the newly independent Greek kingdom. After years of fighting between the Greeks and their Turkish overlords in the Ottoman Empire, the cause of Greek national independence attracted more and more sympathy from Europe's Great Powers. Initially hostile to any change to the settlement for Europe following the 1815 Congress of Vienna, the Great Powers came round to the idea of a fellow Christian monarchy in Europe's South-eastern corner, even if it was at the expense of the Ottoman Empire, the historic buffer against Russian expansion into the Eastern Mediterranean. With the sponsorship of France, Great Britain and Russia, Greek independence was recognised, and the Bavarian prince Otto was selected to establish a Greek monarchy.

Only a teenager at the time of his accession, Otto arrived in Greece with an entourage of Bavarian advisers to help him establish a new Greek government. This would be no easy task, as Greece lacked the infrastructure those in the more developed Western Europe took for granted. Moreover, the young King Otto would have to earn the respect of his new subjects, even though he was a German Catholic now leading a nation predominantly consisting of Orthodox Greeks. As King Otto was initially deemed too young to be making decisions for this new country, he instead relied on his Bavarian court to act on his behalf, which proved controversial with many Greeks. Even once the first few years of his reign had passed, and he was old enough to reign in his own right, King Otto proved to be a controversial figure, exercising most power for himself as an autocratic monarch rather than allowing a Greek government or parliament to make key decisions. To many Greeks, it seemed as though they had just exchanged rule by one group of foreigners for another: from the Ottoman Turks, led by the Sultan, to King Otto and his Bavarian elite, who were in turn being steered by French, British and Russian governments and their respective national interests.

Little over a decade into his reign, King Otto faced a revolution against his rule. In response, he conceded a lot of his political influence, an event marked by the establishment of Constitution Square in Athens, the city that King Otto himself had designated as the capital city of Greece. He nevertheless continued to wield influence over government policy, with his credibility and popularity still undermined by those factors that had hitherto always affected King Otto's standing in Greece: that he was a foreigner who was beholden to Europe's Great Powers, rather than Greece's national interests. This was perhaps most starkly demonstrated during the Crimean War: the first armed conflict between the Great Powers since the Napoleonic Wars. This war pitted the Russian Empire against the Ottoman Empire, with the latter backed by Great Britain and France which, for Greece, meant that the countries she relied upon for financial and other means of support were now fighting amongst themselves. For Greece's national interest, King Otto decided it would be best for his kingdom to take sides and support Russia; the idea being that, if Russia won this war, as a reward for her support Greece could draw into her borders more islands within the region that were populated by Greeks, at the expense of the Ottoman Empire. However, King Otto's stance promptly resulted in national humiliation, as the French and British navies blockaded Greek ports, preventing Greek involvement in the Crimean War, and forcing Greece to reluctantly stay out of the conflict.

Ultimately, despite his reign enduring for several decades, King Otto never succeeded in ingratiating himself enough with his Greek subjects. King Otto was unable to shake off the numerous negative connotations linked with his rule: his difference in religion and nationality, and that of his closest advisers as well, compared with most of his people; his willingness to resort to authoritarian rule at the expense of the democratic principles historically associated with Greek culture; and his repeated displays of impotence when he attempted to oversee policies that worked counter to the interests of the Great Powers. King Otto faced a further revolution in 1862, one from which his regime would not recover, with Otto subsequently deposed and sent to exile, travelling again by British warship, in his native Bavaria. He would remain there for the last few years of his life.

Now the Great Powers had to once again concern themselves with who should be King of Greece. This time they selected a Danish prince, who would reign as King George I. While King George's reign would oversee more stability and progress in Greece, with the Great Powers now wisely abstaining from the sort of interference in the country that had undermined King Otto, his 50-year rule was brought to an abrupt end by his assassination in 1913. Greece would have a rocky twentieth century, not only because it shared the experience of two world wars like other European countries, but also because she went through the regional conflict of the Balkan Wars in the build-up to the First World War; then Greece endured prolonged fighting after the Second World War, as this conflict evolved into the Greek Civil War. Meanwhile, far from providing the sort of stability and continuity that the institution of monarchy is often praised for, Greece's kings in the twentieth century instead seemed to personify their country's turmoil. Following King George I's assassination was the reign of his son, King Constantine I, which was interrupted by the brief reign of his own son King Alexander I, who died after only three years on the throne from a monkey bite. National humiliation in Greece's war with Turkey during King Constantine I's second reign prompted his abdication once and for all, to be replaced by his other son, the controversial King George II, who encouraged military dictatorship in his country and whose reign was interrupted by a short-lived republic.

While the reign of King George II's brother and successor, King Paul, saw Greece through the Civil War, whereby the royalists triumphed over the communists, celebrations of this victory would be short-lived. King Constantine II, King Paul's son and successor, inherited the throne in 1964, at the height of the Cold War. As one of the few capitalist regimes in Eastern Europe, perhaps some in Greece were prone to feeling more paranoid about the communist threat than most in other capitalist democracies at this time. So when a left-wing government was democratically elected during his reign, King Constantine II was persuaded that this marked a precursor to a potential communist takeover, prompting the King to support a coup and military dictatorship in order to depose the left wingers. King Constantine II soon regretted this decision, but the damage was done. Whilst the military established their authoritarian government, King Constantine II went into exile and would never return as king. After the fall of the military dictatorship, a referendum in 1974 comfortably resulted in the selection of a republic over the monarchy, and Greece has remained a republic ever since, thus ending the last surviving monarchy in Eastern Europe. However, while King Constantine II was not the first European monarch to fall after supporting a military dictatorship in difficult times, he would perhaps be the last.

Victoria

The accession of the young Victoria as Queen of the United Kingdom of Great Britain and Ireland in 1837 would have been refreshing for many, following the reigns of her uninspiring uncles, first King George IV then King William IV. King William IV was able to die with a feeling of greater ease because he lived just long enough to see the eighteenth birthday of Victoria, which meant that, when she became Queen, she could reign in her own right, rather than under a regency led by her mother, Princess Victoria, who King William IV despised. In fact, King William IV openly said that he hoped to live long enough so that any royal interference from his hated sister-in-law could be avoided.

Soon after Queen Victoria's accession, popular attention turned to who she would marry, offering her prospective suitor the opportunity to play a role in shaping what was now arguably the most powerful country in the world. Though there were a number of contenders, including the future Tsar Alexander II of Russia, in this endeavour Queen Victoria's uncle, King Leopold I of the Belgians, the first monarch of a newly independent Belgium, managed to get his own way, successfully pushing his niece in the direction of his nephew, Prince Albert of Saxe-Coburg-Gotha. Though only a small German state, Saxe-Coburg-Gotha was now punching above its weight as a steady supplier of royals across the continent. As King Leopold had hoped, the cousins Queen Victoria and Prince Albert fell deeply in love with each other, which in turn would now empower the House of Saxe-Coburg-Gotha's position in Great Britain in addition to Belgium.

Though the concept of constitutional monarchy, with a restricted monarch overseeing a powerful, elected government, was now well entrenched in Great Britain, for a long time the country's monarchs still liked to occasionally intervene in politics, with mixed results. Rather than being impartial, Queen Victoria would often take sides in British politics. Whilst this involvement wasn't always welcomed by her prime ministers, Queen Victoria's relationships with other national leaders (who, often due to the intermarriage between Europe's royal houses, tended to be family members as well) would sometimes prove to be helpful. With Great Britain's frequent opponent, France, Queen Victoria encouraged particular warmth and constructive ties. She had a close relationship, and fostered an alliance with, King Louis Philippe of the French. Even his controversial successor, Emperor Napoleon III, viewed with much suspicion across Europe, was able to enjoy an often good relationship with his British counterpart, a partnership that proved to be advantageous for both Great Britain and France when they were allies during the Crimean War. It was this event in fact that prompted the establishment of an enduring royal legacy: the awarding of the Victoria Cross medal for bravery.

Fortunately for Great Britain's politicians, Queen Victoria's ability to interfere in politics was hindered by the amount of time she would spend childbearing during her early reign, resulting in nine children. This did however create an opening for involvement from Prince Albert, of whom many in the British establishment were suspicious. Queen Victoria was nevertheless very happy for Prince Albert to play an active role in royal duties and bringing up their children, as he could do no wrong in her eyes. The royal couple proved to be a strong partnership, with Prince Albert keen to promote their image as an ideal family and role models to the nation, as opposed to Queen Victoria's womanising predecessors, with Kings George IV and William IV renowned for having mistresses. For a time, Queen Victoria and Prince Albert would be associated with Great Britain's successes and wanted to personify the country's power: from their role in celebrating victory in the Crimean War, to their opening of the Great Exhibition at the Crystal Palace, a showcase of new technology that would help establish the ritual of world exhibitions that endures to the present day.

The world of Queen Victoria was turned upside down by the death of her beloved Prince Albert in 1861, with the Queen adopting black attire and pledging to spend the rest of her life in mourning. Most of the public seemed sympathetic but, when this grief manifested itself in a withdrawal from public appearances and duties, this sympathy began to evaporate and people increasingly questioned the value of a monarch who no longer outwardly seemed to do anything for her country. In one mocking example of this public mood, a sign was hung by a protester outside of Buckingham Palace which read "these commanding premises to be let or sold in consequence of the late occupant's declining business". This feeling became increasingly dangerous for the Queen's position in 1871, with some in Great Britain inspired by revolutionary events taking place at the time in France, and wondering whether they should carry out some sort of revolution of their own in the United Kingdom and install a British republic.

Queen Victoria was encouraged back into public life, and endeared to the masses once again, thanks in part to the cajoling and schmoozing of one of her prime ministers, Benjamin Disraeli. Known as a charmer with a way with words, Disraeli played on the Queen's ego and said that, when it came to flattering royalty, you should lay it on with a trowel. Part of Disraeli's electoral success was down to playing to public feelings of patriotism, trumpeting Great Britain's status as a leading imperial power, which he encouraged Queen Victoria's image as the embodiment of. This was perhaps demonstrated most clearly when he promulgated the law that recognised Queen Victoria as Empress of India, a move that particularly endeared the Queen to him as it meant that she could now be regarded as the equal in precedence to the emperors of Germany, Russia and Austria-Hungary. Queen Victoria's affection for the Conservative Disraeli was matched in strength by her contempt for his Liberal rival, William Gladstone, whose government she described as one of the worst she'd had, complaining that Gladstone's loud and patronising way of speaking to her made her feel as if she was 'a public meeting'. Despite her still occasional interference in politics, Queen Victoria was reassured that she had recovered her position in the nation's affections when one of the numerous assassination attempts on her resulted in an outpouring of public support, prompting the Queen to say that it was "worth being shot at, to see how much one is loved".

By these later years in her reign, Queen Victoria had become an iconic figure. In terms of the British Empire, she was the personification of this institution that stretched across the globe and upon which the sun famously never set as the largest empire in history, touching every continent: from British Guiana in South America, to Canada in North America; from the almost unbroken extent of territory across Africa that reached from the Cape on the southern coast to Cairo on the north coast; then in Asia-Pacific, there were Australia, Malaya, Singapore, and the much-cited jewel in the Empire's crown, India, to name a few of her territories. Pomp and ceremony was rolled out in Great Britain and across the Empire for her golden jubilee in 1887, then again for her diamond jubilee a decade later. Meanwhile, closer to home, she was regarded as Europe's grandmother, given that her children and grandchildren had married into numerous different royal households across the continent (see Appendix II), which meant that royal family occasions at this time, from christenings and weddings to jubilees and funerals, also resembled international summits, of which Queen Victoria positioned herself as head.

However, at the turn of the twentieth century, both Queen Victoria and her country appeared to be more fragile. Despite Great Britain's trumpeted strength, it was difficult to ignore those now increasingly capable to displace her position at the top, from the nearby rival of Germany, to the upstart powers emerging from outside of Europe such as the United States and Japan. Great Britain's signs of weakness were exposed in the Boer War in South Africa which, although ultimately resulting in British victory, had proven to be remarkably difficult for her to win, despite her considerable resources being pinned against a relatively small band of Boer farmers. Great Britain's conduct in the War also drew widespread criticism, with Queen Victoria's grandson, Emperor Wilhelm II of Germany, one of the most vocal critics. Queen Victoria would not live to see Great Britain's eventual victory, passing away in 1901, a year before the War ended, with her controversial grandson Emperor Wilhelm II at her bedside. Thus ended what, up until that point, had been the longest reign of the oldest monarch ever in the British Isles, and marked the end of a dramatic era in British history.

Franz Joseph

The fortunes of Austria, and the European order it played a leading role in forging, changed drastically in the time from the Congress of Vienna in 1815 to the accession of Franz Joseph as Emperor of Austria in 1848. Together the shrewd leaders of Austria in 1815, Emperor Francis I and his chancellor, Klemens von Metternich, played a dominant role amongst the Great Powers as hosts of the Congress of Vienna, summoned in response to the Napoleonic Wars. During this prolonged summit, Europe's powers effectively redrew the map to, on the one hand, try to erase many of the changes brought about by the French Revolution of 1789 and subsequent Napoleonic Wars while, on the other hand, sculpt the continent to suit their respective national interests. Thus, the leaders connived to install and reinstall leaders and borders that they supported, with the hope of bringing stability to the continent, and for most countries to be effectively ruled by a single, extended family, that was interconnected thanks to generations of inter-breeding amongst European royal families.

This settlement endured for some time, but the warning signs of popular dissatisfaction with this setup were dramatically exposed by the pockets of revolution in 1830, as seen in France and what would become Belgium and Poland. Then, just as European revolutions were triggered by events in France in 1830, so the same would happen again, on a greater scale, in 1848, when King Louis Philippe was forced from the French throne. Meanwhile, the negative side of those tight-knit family ties among European royalty seemed to be personified in the man unfortunate enough to be leading the Austrian Empire in the year of European revolutions. Emperor Francis was by this time long gone and the Austrian throne had been inherited by his son, who became Emperor Ferdinand. However, given how closely related Emperor Ferdinand's parents were (first cousins in two ways), it is suspected that there was too little new blood within the Emperor, which could explain why Emperor Ferdinand was plagued by debilitating health conditions, not least experiencing epileptic seizures on a frequent basis. Moreover, though Emperor Ferdinand married another royal, Princess Maria Anna of Savoy (the royal family of the north-western Italian Kingdom of Piedmont-Sardinia), they were unable to produce children due to the plentiful health problems of the Emperor. It is said that attempts to consummate their marriage led the Emperor to experience even more seizures than usual.

Although the fragile Emperor and his country were still guided by Chancellor Metternich they were overwhelmed by the 1848 revolutions, with several of the nationalities within the cosmopolitan Austrian Empire inspired to rebel and demand greater freedom from their Habsburg rulers, not least the Empire's sizable Hungarian population. As Emperor Ferdinand struggled on through the crisis, Chancellor Metternich's career came to an ignominious end as he fled the Austrian capital, Vienna, apparently carried away whilst hiding inside a laundry cart. Mindful that the survival of the Austrian Empire could be at stake, Emperor Ferdinand was compelled to abdicate in favour of his sprightly young nephew, the 18-year-old Franz Joseph. Troops were dispersed across the Empire to restore order, with significant success, but the threat posed by Hungarian nationalists, led by Lajos Kossuth, endured. To overcome the threat, Emperor Franz Joseph called upon his fellow conservative monarch, Tsar Nicholas I of Russia, to send troops to reinforce those of Austria to suppress Kossuth's movement for Hungarian self-government. Tsar Nicholas responded to the young emperor's plea: a cause for celebration for the new Emperor Franz Joseph, but would be a brutal experience for the Hungarian nationalists involved. Emperor Franz Joseph's handling of the revolution, and ability to forcefully regain control of the Empire, promptly gave him the reputation of a strong yet ruthless ruler. However, the fact that the Austrian Empire had been threatened so drastically by the 1848 revolutions, and had had to call upon another power to restore order, exposed its weakness.

Chancellor Metternich's departure during the course of the 1848 revolutions seemed to symbolise the end of the order he helped create at the Congress of Vienna; a development reinforced by the breakdown of unity between Europe's Great Powers demonstrated just five years later when the Crimean War broke out between them, with Great Britain and France fighting against Russia. The Austrian Empire largely avoided this conflict, but couldn't help being drawn into the nationalist wars later in the 1850s and into the 1860s, which resulted in the unification and establishment of first the Kingdom of Italy then the Empire of Germany, both happening at the expense of Austrian territory and influence. Austria's humiliating defeat against the Kingdom of Prussia in the Austro-Prussian War put great pressure on Emperor Franz Joseph to reform his country. So, in 1867, rather than continuing to suppress Hungarian calls for greater independence, Emperor Franz Joseph oversaw a great U-turn known as the Ausgleich, whereby the Empire would be split in two. Known thereafter as Austria-Hungary, Hungary would now be on a level-footing with Austria, with a separate government responsible for their half of the Empire and the various peoples that lived within it. Nevertheless, Franz Joseph would continue to act as a unifying figure, holding the positions of both Emperor of Austria and King of Hungary.

The combination of a downgrade in Austria-Hungary's international status, and the inevitable impact of ageing, saw Emperor Franz Joseph's image change from that of a powerful young autocrat to more of an endearing and wise grandfather figure. Exploiting the fact that there was no title regarded in higher precedence than emperor, it is said that Emperor Franz Joseph, in order to avoid lengthy meetings, used to insist on taking part in all meetings standing up. Due to the Emperor's high status, etiquette meant that no-one could sit down unless Emperor Franz Joseph did, which meant that everyone was obliged to stand for as long as him. Consequently, the discomfort this caused for visitors tended to encourage those Emperor Franz Joseph was meeting to keep their comments brief and concise. In his later years, Emperor Franz Joseph attracted a lot of sympathy due to the numerous family tragedies he was exposed to: first was the mysterious death, believed to be by suicide, of his son and heir, Crown Prince Rudolf, and his mistress; then the Emperor's wife, Empress Elisabeth, informally known as Sisi, was assassinated just under a decade later.

Another family tragedy for Emperor Franz Joseph, which would infamously have far-reaching consequences, was the assassination of his heir and nephew,

Archduke Franz Ferdinand, in 1914. Archduke Franz Ferdinand died at the hands of a Serbian nationalist during a visit to Bosnia, a territory which had a large Serb population yet, due to European power politics, had quite recently been controversially added to the Austro-Hungarian Empire rather than the Kingdom of Serbia. The Archduke's assassination motivated Emperor Franz Joseph and his government to hold the whole Serbian nation responsible, and declared war on Serbia. In defence of her Serbian ally, Russia mobilised her troops against Austria-Hungary, so Germany in turn declared war on Russia, in support of her Habsburg ally. Then, as an ally of Russia, France was obliged to declare war on Germany. Great Britain had a loose alliance with France and Russia, and was unsure of whether to become directly involved or not. However, when Germany's military strategy involved invading Belgium, whose sovereignty Great Britain had guaranteed to uphold, Great Britain consequently declared war on Germany, all of which marking the beginning of the First World War, known at the time as the Great War.

Although Emperor Franz Joseph had led his country into this war, he privately shared his concerns with his family that Austria-Hungary, which already showed signs of disunity because of the divergent nationalities it had and their respective experiences under imperial rule, may not survive the conflict and could ultimately break-up. Emperor Franz Joseph would not live to see if his prophecy would come true, as he died half way through the War in 1916, leaving the very unenviable position of attempting to see Austria-Hungary through the conflict to his great-nephew, the new Emperor Karl.

Napoleon

When Louis Napoleon Bonaparte was elected as first President of the Second French Republic (established in the wake of the 1848 revolutions), it was largely thanks to nostalgia associated with his iconic uncle, the former Emperor Napoleon I of the French. It is therefore perhaps not altogether too surprising that, with all the romance and adventure associated with the House of Bonaparte, Louis Napoleon felt that in 1852, just a few years into his presidency, he could get away with overthrowing the republic he was elected to lead. He transformed the Second Republic into the Second French Empire, and crowned himself Emperor Napoleon III of the French. Interestingly, just as his Bourbon predecessors had recognised the uncrowned King Louis XVII of France, Emperor Napoleon III recognised the son of Emperor Napoleon I as the uncrowned Emperor Napoleon II.

The return of a Napoleonic regime in France would no doubt have concerned Europe's other Great Powers, but Emperor Napoleon III reassured them that he had no intention of going on a continent-wide campaign of conquest like his uncle half a century before. Nevertheless, he was keen to have an active foreign policy, with the onset of the Crimean War providing Emperor Napoleon III with his first great opportunity to prove himself as worthy of the name Napoleon. Though it was a difficult victory for France and her British allies, in defence of the Ottoman Empire against Russia, it was a victory nonetheless, which gave

Emperor Napoleon III the boost he had hoped for. This was aided further by the prestige gained from Emperor Napoleon III hosting the post-war settlement and signing of the Treaty of Paris. One of the other outcomes of the Crimean War was the relationship Emperor Napoleon III was able to establish with Count Cavour, Prime Minister of the Kingdom of Piedmont-Sardinia, a country which covered Piedmont in the northwest of the Italian peninsula, and the relatively large Mediterranean island of Sardinia. At this time the Italian peninsula was fragmented and, other than Piedmont-Sardinia, was divided into broadly three areas. The north was dominated by the Habsburg dynasty, with a large part of the region falling within the borders of the Austrian Empire, whilst the rest of the region largely consisted of smaller states ruled by other Habsburgs. In the south was the Kingdom of Two Sicilies, which also included the island of Sicily, ruled by the Bourbons, and consequently enjoyed close family ties with other European royals, not least with their fellow Bourbons that ruled France and Spain. Then at the centre of the Italian peninsula were the Papal States, ruled personally by the Pope. Despite these divisions there was a common (if vague) Italian language, historic associations with the empire of Ancient Rome, and, of course, geography.

In this age of nationalism, there were some ambitions for all Italians to be united in one country, potentially to be ruled by the King of Piedmont-Sardinia, the Pope or as a republic. However, with the Papacy unsympathetic to the concept, expectations for a united Italy rested upon Piedmont-Sardinia. Count Cavour shared his ambitions with Emperor Napoleon III to govern a united Northern Italy (deliberately excluding the poorer south), and the two concluded a deal: France would back Piedmont-Sardinia in a war with Austria that would force the Habsburgs out of the region, and allow Piedmont-Sardinia's House of Savoy to take their place. In exchange France would be given Nice and Savoy, and the House of Bonaparte's royal credentials would be boosted by an arranged marriage between Emperor Napoleon III's cousin to a daughter of Piedmont-Sardinia's King Victor Emmanuel II. In addition, Emperor Napoleon III hoped that association with the unification of Italy would contribute to his lasting legacy in Europe.

In 1859 the war was duly begun, and appeared to be going in Piedmont-Sardinia's favour. However, Cavour was shocked by an unusually cautious act by Emperor Napoleon III: he withdrew his support for the war prematurely, concluding a peace agreement with Emperor Franz Joseph of Austria before enough Italian territory had been taken to fully realise Cavour's ambitions. Consequently, France's contribution to Italian unification wasn't as great as had been expected, with the rest of the process largely down to the efforts of the Italians themselves: Cavour's north Italian kingdom was by now largely established, with referenda leading to the other Italian territories in the region coming under Piedmont-Sardinia's King Victor Emmanuel II. In an unexpected twist, the Italian nationalist adventurer, Giuseppe Garibaldi, saw this as an opportunity to unite the entire peninsula, and led an army of volunteers that toppled the Kingdom of Two Sicilies. Garibaldi then marched on the Papal States, which caused concern for the new Italian kingdom: the Pope had powerful backing across Europe, so if he was deemed to be in danger, the fledgling Italian cause could make some influential enemies elsewhere on the continent. King Victor Emmanuel II therefore personally rode out on horseback to meet Garibaldi to deter a direct attack on the Pope, a meeting which resulted in their respective territories being brought together to make the Kingdom of Italy. However, for the time being at least, the Kingdom of Italy would not include Rome, which would remain under the Pope.

Emperor Napoleon III's foreign policy continued to be active, but increasingly worked against him. Taking advantage of instability in North America resulting from the American Civil War, Emperor Napoleon III set about backing a pro-French Mexican Empire, and supporting Maximilian, brother of Emperor Franz Joseph of Austria, as its new emperor. However, the Mexican Empire failed to firmly establish itself and was abolished after only a few years, and in 1867 Emperor Maximilian was executed by a Mexican firing squad. Moreover, it was around this time that a secret deal discussed by Emperor Napoleon III and King William III of the Netherlands, whereby Luxembourg would potentially be sold by the Dutch to France, was made public, with the Second French Empire now firmly seen as Europe's troublemaker. The shrewd chancellor of the Kingdom of Prussia, Otto von Bismarck, was able to see and exploit this. In the 1860s, Prussia had gone from strength to strength by winning, first, the War of Schleswig-Holstein, and then the Austro-Prussian War, which resulted in Prussia annexing a number of smaller German states and effectively replacing Austria as Europe's foremost Germanic power. Bismarck then succeeded in his final step, which was to provoke a war between Prussia and France, whereby France would receive no backing from the other Great Powers due to their suspicion of Emperor Napoleon III and his ambitions. At the turn of the 1870s, the Franco-Prussian War resulted in a Prussian victory, with Prussian troops humiliatingly marching into France. To add insult to injury, the peace agreement was concluded in the French Palace of Versailles in 1871.

At the same occasion, the Empire of Germany was declared, consisting of 25 states, of which Prussia would be by far the largest and most dominant. Otto von Bismarck would be Germany's chancellor, while Prussia's King Wilhelm I now became the first Emperor of Germany. Interestingly, whilst the earlier unification of Italy had meant the deposition of all Italian royals except for King Victor Emmanuel II, the German Empire preserved many of the other German monarchies. This meant that, while Wilhelm I became Emperor of Germany, he remained King of Prussia as well. Other German monarchs, such as the kings of Bavaria and Wurttemberg, would also maintain their thrones; albeit, now subordinate to the German Emperor. Meanwhile, in the face of this humiliation, Emperor Napoleon III was compelled to relinquish the French imperial throne, and spent the last couple of years of his life in exile in Great Britain. And once again France was left to decide where to turn next for leadership.

Alexander

Tsar Alexander II of Russia had an unenviable inheritance when he ascended the throne in 1855, with his country approaching defeat in the Crimean War, a conflict fought on Russian soil. Defeat on home ground was a great comedown for the empire that, early in the nineteenth century, had pushed Emperor Napoleon and his armies all the way from Moscow and across Europe into Paris, with the armies of Tsar Alexander I marching triumphantly into the French capital. Then his younger brother and successor, Tsar Nicholas I, gained a reputation as Europe's policeman for his defence of the conservative order in the continent, as greatly demonstrated when he propped up the young Emperor Franz Joseph's Austrian Empire during the 1848 revolutions. But since then, Tsar Nicholas I had led his country unsuccessfully through the Crimean War, and it was left to his son and successor, Tsar Alexander II, to handle the consequences of defeat.

Seeing widespread rebellion against the conservative order in Europe in 1848, and now the defeat of perhaps Europe's most conservative regime, the Russian Empire, Tsar Alexander II's response was to implement radical reforms to revitalise his country. Throughout the 1860s, Tsar Alexander II began to bring about these changes, one of the earliest and most radical being the abolition of serfdom. Serfdom was a life comparable to slavery that a large portion of the Russian population endured. This was a characteristic of society that was by this time exceptional to Russia, which the new tsar believed should be abolished to aid his country's advancement. Doing so would make Russia more like the other European nations in this regard, though such a drastic change as emancipation of the serfs would have far-reaching consequences, both good and bad. Freedom had its obvious virtues for those who had serfdom imposed on them, and it was also felt that changing serfs into paid labour with their own spending power could boost the national economy. But former serfs now found they had responsibilities for their own wellbeing which they were hitherto unused to and would struggle to adjust to, whilst landowners suddenly required additional funds to pay for the workers on their land. Nevertheless, in the eyes of posterity, this was seen as an important step in the evolution of Russian society, with Tsar Alexander II to be known as 'the Liberator'.

In addition, Tsar Alexander II took Russia on some of her earliest steps down what would be a long and very unsteady path towards democracy. He initiated zemstvos, which were local governing bodies elected by the public. Meanwhile in Finland, amongst Russia's newest and most peripheral territories, of which Tsar Alexander II was Grand Duke, the nation's record of peace and stability was rewarded by Tsar Alexander II through his restoration of Finland's own parliamentary body, the Finnish Diet. His relatively benign rule of Finland, and continued respect of its ability to govern itself, earned Tsar Alexander II a positive reputation amongst his Finnish subjects. However, despite his liberal reputation among many of his subjects, as well as overseas observers, the same could not be said for his reputation in his Polish and Lithuanian territories. In response to nationalist unrest in these lands, Tsar Alexander II resorted to the traditional Russian imperial tactic of oppression, and rescinded the degree of Polish self-government previously in place.

During his reign, the measures Tsar Alexander II took often tended to blend pragmatic attempts to improve his country, yet also implicitly recognised Russia's vulnerability. This was well demonstrated when he authorised the sale of Russia's Alaskan territory. During a time when European empires were generally looking to expand, it seemed to be an unusual move for Russia to willingly concede territory. The sale of Alaska by Tsar Alexander II to the United States of America would have undoubtedly given state funds a boost, but there was a strategic motivation behind this decision as well. Situated in the north-western corner of North America, although Alaska was just across the Bering Strait from the vast expanse of the Russian Empire that stretched the length of

Asia and into Eastern Europe, it also bordered the immense British territory of Canada. As Alaska shared an extensive border with Canada, it was at great risk of potential invasion and conquest by Britain, Russia's great imperial rival, via Canada. Considering attempts to boost the defences of Alaska impractical and undesirable, it was deemed to be more practical to cede this territory to the USA instead, and achieve a boost to the national coffers at the same time. Nevertheless, implicit in this decision was a recognition of weakness when confronted by British power. What Tsar Alexander II wouldn't have anticipated though was that, by authorising this decision, he had encouraged the territorial expansion of the country that would, a century later, be the greatest opponent to his nation during the course of the Cold War.

Neither Tsar Alexander II's repeated attempts to reform and develop Russia, nor victory in the Russo-Turkish War of the late 1870s (thus reversing Russia's humiliation in the earlier Crimean War), appeared to stifle that relentless threat confronted by many national leaders, most apparent in the nineteenth century: the threat of assassination. Numerous attempts were made on his life during his reign and, whilst Tsar Alexander II continued to pursue reforms, these attempts at change did not reduce the frequency of these attempts, if anything, they increased. As such, throughout his reign the Tsar vacillated between implementing reforms on the one hand, and resorting to traditional Tsarist oppression on the other, in an effort to maintain order and minimise criticism of his rule. So relentless were the attempts on his life, Tsar Alexander II went from being able to walk freely alone through the streets of St Petersburg to requiring constant protection from armed bodyguards when in public. Towards the end of his reign, it was said that he felt so constrained that he was like a prisoner within his own palaces.

At the turn of the 1880s, Tsar Alexander II began to consult with Russia's political leaders on further drastic measures to deter these attempts and placate his opponents. In collaboration with Russian minister, Count Loris-Melikov, Tsar Alexander II began to piece together plans to introduce a national parliament. However, before these plans could be put into practice, one of the many assassination attempts against the Tsar finally succeeded in 1881, stopping these plans in their tracks, or at least delaying them. Whilst travelling through St Petersburg in his carriage one day, political activists threw explosives at Tsar Alexander II, one of which inflicting fatal injuries upon him. The death of Tsar Alexander II brought about a complete change in attitude among his successors on the Russia throne: first his son, Tsar Alexander III, then his grandson, Tsar Nicholas II. Seeing the many significant reforms implemented by Tsar Alexander II on the one hand, and relentless attempts on his life throughout his reign on the other, his successors came to the conclusion that there was no public gratitude for these reforms, and if anything, resulted in a loss of respect for the Russian monarchy, as well as power. So far as they saw it, the traditional Russian leadership style of autocratic governance deployed by previous tsars had produced the greatest successes for Russia, while democracy only undermined national stability. Therefore, Tsars Alexander III and Nicholas II oversaw a return to autocratic rule; though the challenges faced by the Tsar Liberator would resurface in Russia in the years ahead.

Henri

When Emperor Napoleon III of the French was forced to forfeit the French throne in 1871, there was a good chance that he would be succeeded as the French head of state by a King Henri V of France, otherwise known as Henri, Count of Chambord, and grandson of the last King of France, King Charles X. After all, there was a conservative consensus within the French establishment at the time, desiring stability in the wake of France's humiliating defeat in the Franco-Prussian War.

The nineteenth century had hitherto been a changeable one for France, with the list of systems of government there since the French Revolution reminiscent of the Twelve Days of Christmas: three Bourbon monarchs, two French republics, two Bonapartist empires, and a king from the House of Orleans. France's exposure to this variety of systems, each with their perceived strengths and weaknesses, consequently attracted their own supporters, drastically dividing French politics.

At this time there were four powerful political movements in France. There were the Legitimists, who backed the restoration of the Bourbon dynasty and tended to be socially conservative, thus mirroring the outlook of the man they sponsored as a prospective national leader, Henri of Chambord. On the other hand, the Orleanists supported the claim to the French throne of Prince Philippe,

Count of Paris and grandson of the former King Louis Philippe of the French, and tended to be more liberal, advocating a constitutional monarchy, i.e., a largely symbolic monarchy that oversaw a powerful but democratic parliament. Meanwhile, although significantly discredited at this time by the fact that France's military defeat had been overseen by Emperor Napoleon III, he still had his supporters, and Bonapartists also looked to his son as a prospective Emperor Napoleon IV. Then, finally, there were the republicans, with examples of successful republics existing outside of Europe to look to as role models, notably the increasingly prominent United States of America. In France though, republicanism was still associated by many with the anarchic first republic established after the 1789 revolution, then the short-lived second republic overthrown by Emperor Napoleon III. The prevailing conservative consensus at this time, as reflected by the preponderance of monarchist politicians in power, therefore appeared to tilt towards a restoration of France as a kingdom, though were divided as to whether Henri or Philippe should be counted upon as the head of state France needed during these unstable times. To the relief of contemporary politicians, a compromise emerged that seemed palatable to both Legitimists and Orleanists, thus appealing to a considerable portion of influential members of French society. To satisfy Legitimists, Henri could indeed be crowned King of France, and reign for the rest of his life. However, by the time of his prospective accession, Count Henri had reached middle-age and remained childless. As such, he was considered very unlikely to ever produce any offspring. Consequently, with his death in the foreseeable future, and with the French Bourbon dynasty by then extinct and the Legitimist cause severely hampered, Henri could be succeeded by Prince Philippe, or whoever happened to be Orleanist claimant by that time, as King. This deal attracted considerable support that, crucially, included the cautious backing of Counts Henri and Philippe.

However, as Count Henri and France's leading politicians began to negotiate the form this new Kingdom of France should take, the process was brought to a halt by a seemingly small, but symbolically important, obstacle: the national flag. Historically, and tracing back to the Bourbon restoration earlier in the nineteenth century, France's flag had been one that was strongly tied with the House of Bourbon: the fleur de lis on a white background. However, for much of the nineteenth century, this had been replaced by the red, white and blue tricolour, as implemented by the French republics, empires and Orleanist monarchy, and as such had become synonymous with modern France. As a Bourbon, and a conservative one at that, Count Henri said he would only reign in a France over which the fleur de lis flew. This was rejected by the politicians, who insisted on the tricolour. The tricolour symbolised modern France, a relatively liberal country, that had united republicans, Orleanists and Bonapartists alike; as opposed to the more anachronistic connotations of the fleur de lis, which seemed to imply a rejection of the many changes and developments in France since 1789, and thus suggested a desire to forget everything about the numerous versions of the country that the public had grown used to in that time. This resulted in a stalemate, with nether side wanting to back down, based on the principles each flag represented.

A new compromise was then forged: a republic would be temporarily introduced and then, by the time the overly-conservative Count Henri had died, a more liberal monarchy could be installed to replace it under the House of Orleans, which would hopefully attract support from Legitimists as well as Orleanists. This compromise was personified by Adolphe Thiers, a conservative politician with monarchist sympathies who was nevertheless elected as the first President of this new republic, whose most famous words were his description of the Third French Republic as a means to a government that "divides us the least". However, by the time Count Henri duly passed away in 1883, this new republic had managed to avoid the guillotining associated with the first republic's reign of terror, and at the same time did not succumb to Bonapartist nostalgia like the second republic. Instead, by this time at least, the third republic had brought relative stability to France. As such, the restoration of the monarchy again was put on ice and this temporary republican France, albeit with a number of changes, has continued to this day. Republicans through the generations could raise their glasses to Count Henri, who had apparently done so much to deter the restoration of the monarchy in France, and inadvertently ushered in an enduring republic.

Nikola

When Russia achieved victory in the Russo-Turkish War in 1878, Tsar Alexander II was not the only royal to celebrate this outcome. Defeat had resulted in the loss of significant territory for the Ottoman Turks, much of which would be recognised as the newly-independent principalities of Serbia, Romania and, fortunately for Prince Nikola of the Petrovic-Njegos dynasty, his country of Montenegro too. Whilst the Ottoman Empire had been on the winning side in the Crimean War against Russia decades before, this time the Ottomans lacked the crucial backing of Great Britain and France. If anything, these countries were amongst the numerous nations responsible for the dismembering of the Ottoman Empire. Increasingly referred to as 'the sick man of Europe', the Ottomans had lost Algeria to France in recent decades, whilst British Prime Minister Benjamin Disraeli negotiated his country's acquisition of Cyprus from the Ottomans in the wake of their 1878 defeat. The Ottoman Empire had historically been able to rely on support from at least some of the Great Powers because it was seen as a useful buffer against expansion of the Russian Empire and was valued for its role in the European balance of power. Ironically, Disraeli had long been one of the greatest advocates of the Ottoman Turks for this reason. Though the independence of Greece had been a significant loss of territory and influence for the Ottomans in Europe, France and Great Britain stood by her during the Crimean War. Afterwards however, the combination of the continued decline of Ottoman power (and consequently of her strategic value as well) since then, and her controversial treatment of the Christian minorities within this Islamic Empire (not least of the Empire's Bulgarians), led to the Ottoman Empire losing crucial sympathy and support from the Great Powers.

As the Ottomans' grip on South-eastern Europe, a region known as the Balkans due to the Balkan Mountains found there, ebbed back towards its hub around present-day Turkey, new countries were able to emerge in its wake. These countries were not artificial constructs though, but reflections of distinct and long-established nations camouflaged by Ottoman rule. In the case of Montenegro, it had existed for centuries as a self-governing, peripheral territory of the Ottoman Empire, shielded and obscured by the black mountains that gave the nation its name. The traditional link between religion and royalty was encapsulated in Montenegro by the title used by her historic national leaders, known as Prince-Bishops, with the home-grown House of Petrovic-Njegos long holding this position. In the nineteenth century the religious part of their title was dropped, with Nikola inheriting the title of Prince of Montenegro in 1860, though he would not receive international recognition as Montenegro's head of state until the end of the Russo-Turkish War 18 years later. During the course of his reign, Prince Nikola would oversee a number of developments for the Montenegrin nation in addition to the achievement of total independence, notably introducing Montenegro's first constitution. Then in 1910, to celebrate his own golden jubilee, Nikola elevated the status of Montenegro from a principality to a kingdom, and consequently his own title from Prince to King.

Montenegro was quite noteworthy in Europe for retaining her indigenous dynasty, the House of Petrovic-Njegos, when many other countries had imported German royals to become their heads of state. Nevertheless, this did not prevent King Nikola from integrating the Montenegrin royal family into the web of family ties stretching across Europe. In fact, so successful was he in this endeavour that he came to be known as the 'father-in-law of Europe', as two of his daughters married Russian royals, while another daughter married the future King Victor Emmanuel III of Italy. Meanwhile the existing bonds between Montenegro and Serbia, as neighbours and fellow Orthodox Christian nations that had experienced Ottoman rule, were reinforced by the marriage of King Nikola's daughter, Princess Zorka, to Prince Peter of the Karadjordjevic dynasty. Peter would become King of Serbia in 1903, following the murder of Serbia's King Alexander of the rival Obrenovic dynasty. In solidarity with King Peter's

Serbia, King Nikola would later rally Montenegro to enter what would become the First World War as their ally. By the end of this conflict, matters would take an ironic twist given King Nikola's personal support for the war effort, as Montenegro's politicians decided it would be more beneficial for their country to join the newly emerging Kingdom of Serbs, Croats and Slovenes, which was to be ruled by Serbia's King Peter. Thus, when Montenegro joined this new country, the now elderly King Nikola was deposed and went into exile in France, where he would die a few years later in 1921 aged 79.

Over the generations, the exiled Montenegrin royal family would maintain a strong connection with France, observing from there the numerous changes experienced by Montenegro as part of the volatile country that would be known for much of the twentieth century as Yugoslavia. When the frailties of Yugoslavia were exposed during the Second World War, as the country was broken up by the Axis Powers, one of the numerous nations proposed by Nazi Germany and Fascist Italy to emerge from Yugoslavia presented an opportunity for the House of Petrovic-Njegos: a new Kingdom of Montenegro under Prince Michael, grandson of King Nikola. However, with the communist dictator Josip Broz Tito promptly binding Yugoslavia back together again after the War, it perhaps seemed unlikely that either an independent Montenegro or its House of Petrovic-Njegos would ever be restored. With the break-up of Yugoslavia once and for all over the 1990s, and the onset of the twenty-first century though, both were about to make a comeback.

In 2006 Montenegro decided in a referendum, albeit by quite a slim majority, to end its union with Serbia and become an independent country again. Curiously, whilst Montenegro became a republic (as had become the norm for countries established and re-established since the First World War), it adopted the House of Petrovic-Njegos' coat of arms as the national flag. Furthermore, in 2011, negotiations between the Montenegrin government and Prince Nikola Petrovic-Njegos, great-grandson of King Nikola of Montenegro and known as Nikola II amongst monarchists, culminated in a remarkable outcome. Good relations were now restored between Montenegro's government and former royal family, resulting in Prince Nikola being invited back to Montenegro from France. Moreover, new legislation spelt out that he would also be asked to perform functions on behalf of the Montenegrin government at home and abroad. This outcome marks the most significant step forward for monarchy in Europe since the restoration of the Spanish monarchy in the 1970s, and in Eastern Europe since the Second World War.

Friedrich

The accession of Emperor Friedrich III of Germany in 1888 encouraged strong feelings, both positive and negative, in his country and beyond. However, 1888 would be Germany's year of three emperors: a fact that would be regarded as a relief to some, and a sadly missed opportunity for others. Since the German Empire had been formed in 1871 as a result of Prussia's victory in the Franco-Prussian War, Emperor Wilhelm I of Germany and his chancellor, Otto von Bismarck, had imposed on their new country the conservative culture they had cultivated in the Kingdom of Prussia beforehand. The two formed a conservative partnership not unlike the one that had existed between Emperor Francis and Chancellor Klemens von Metternich of Austria earlier in the century. Another similarity between these two double acts was that, just as they had upheld conservatism at home, they encouraged it across Europe as well. For much of the 1870s and 1880s, with the backing of Emperor Wilhelm I, Bismarck famously instigated, and endeavoured to safeguard, a web of alliances amongst the Great Powers that would see Germany receiving international support while at the same time isolating her recent enemy, France. Bismarck did so by encouraging the dreikaiserbund, the three emperors' league, which was a conservative alliance between the empires of Germany, Austria-Hungary and Russia. In addition, he pushed for a military alliance between Germany, Austria-Hungary and Italy. Meanwhile, though Great Britain was known at this time for a foreign policy of 'splendid isolation', whereby she avoided alliances with European powers that could drag her into undesired wars, Bismarck nevertheless enjoyed good relations with Britain's Conservative prime ministers.

However, whilst Bismarck was seen by some of Britain's elected leaders as a man who promoted peace and stability, as well as lucrative trade, in Europe, the country's monarch, Queen Victoria, and members of the liberal elite, took a dimmer view of Bismarck and the contempt he appeared to show towards the democratic and liberal values of the United Kingdom. Queen Victoria, and those who shared her wariness of Germany's so-called 'iron chancellor', saw the opportunity for change in the country with the marriage of Prince Friedrich, son and heir to the German throne, to Princess Victoria, Queen Victoria's eldest child. Prince Friedrich had liberal leanings that were greatly encouraged by Princess Victoria, with the royal couple spending a lot of time exposed to Great Britain and the relatively liberal and democratic governance there. It was consequently hoped that they would bring about in Germany the sort of constitutional monarchy that was by now well established in Great Britain. Unsurprisingly, this was not a prospect Otto von Bismarck relished.

There was therefore great interest at the time of Emperor Wilhelm I's death, and Friedrich's accession to Germany's imperial throne, in 1888. Bismarck was able to remain Germany's chancellor, for the time being at least, but feared a significant reduction in his influence at best under his new emperor. The life of Emperor Friedrich III would take a fatal turn however: around the time of his accession, Emperor Friedrich was diagnosed with throat cancer which would prove to be terminal. As the first months of his reign passed, it became clear that Emperor Friedrich III would not live long enough to make the mark on Germany that his supporters and detractors alike had expected. His condition became so bad so quickly that, within a short space of time, Emperor Friedrich III even lost the ability to speak and had to communicate through writing notes instead. Before even a year into his reign could pass, Emperor Friedrich III died, making his son, Emperor Wilhelm II, Germany's third emperor in the space of one year.

Lacking his parents' liberal leanings, Emperor Wilhelm II promptly restored Germany's status as a conservative power. This would by no means mean a return to prominence for Otto von Bismarck though, who clashed with Emperor Wilhelm II, leading Bismarck to resign as German chancellor only a couple of years into his reign. Unfortunately, Bismarck's carefully manipulated system of alliances to protect Germany's otherwise vulnerable location at the heart of Europe fell with him. The dreikaiserbund was allowed to lapse by Emperor

Wilhelm II, leading Tsar Nicholas II's Russia to seek an alliance with France instead, raising the prospect of Germany fighting a war against powerful countries on her eastern and western borders simultaneously, which Bismarck had endeavoured to avoid. Moreover, the capricious Kaiser (Kaiser being the German word for emperor) antagonised Great Britain, criticising her conduct in the Boer War at the turn of the century, and encouraging a military rivalry that would see the two countries trying to outdo one another in a competition to have the world's strongest navy. Emperor Wilhelm II seemed to have a complex view of Great Britain that would in some ways mirror the unusual relationship he had with his British mother. The Kaiser would at times clearly show love for his mother, the former Empress Victoria of Germany; this was sometimes even expressed in a way that would seem to be more sexual than familial. Then again, he would also show great contempt towards her, and side-line her as a traitor for apparently demonstrating more loyalty to her native Britain than Germany. Similarly, there were times when Emperor Wilhelm II seemed to respect and be impressed by British power, but this later appeared to evolve into jealousy and paranoia. There is speculation that his paranoia and unusual behaviour was brought about by self-consciousness of the erb's palsy he was born with, resulting in a deformed arm; a condition he resented and felt was perceived as a sign of weakness.

The seemingly unconditional support Emperor Wilhelm II pledged to Emperor Franz Joseph of Austria-Hungary following Archduke Franz Ferdinand's assassination is often attributed as a leading cause in the escalation of events culminating in the First World War. During the course of the War, Emperor Wilhelm II became the personification of the enemy in propaganda in Great Britain and the other Entente Powers, and consequently made him a focal point for punishment when Germany was defeated. Emperor Wilhelm II managed to avoid retribution with a swift exile to the safety of the Netherlands, whilst Germany's monarchy was abolished and a fragile republic emerged in its place. Little over ten years into its existence, this fledgling republic would be manipulated by Adolf Hitler into perhaps the most infamous regime in history: Nazi Germany.

Wilhelmina

Despite being just a ten-year-old child at her accession in 1890, Queen Wilhelmina of the Netherlands immediately brought about disruption and change, as a consequence of her gender. At the Congress of Vienna in 1815, the newly-appointed King William I of the Netherlands had also been recognised as Luxembourg's first Grand Duke, establishing a personal union between the two countries, though Luxembourg would be largely self-governing. This self-government also extended to Luxembourg having a constitution of her own, which stated that only men could inherit the Luxembourgish throne. Thus, when King William III of the Netherlands died in 1890, his replacement by a Dutch queen meant that, under Luxembourgish law, a male alternative monarch needed to be sought, thus severing the personal union binding the Netherlands and Luxembourg. King William III's distant cousin, Duke Adolphe of Nassau, was selected to establish Luxembourg's own dynasty. Ironically, the new Grand Duke Adolphe of Luxembourg's son and successor, Grand Duke William IV, would only have daughters. Reluctant to trace yet another male heir, and with a male-only succession seeming increasingly archaic in the early twentieth century, Luxembourgish law was changed, which allowed for Grand Duke William IV's two successors to be women: his daughters, the Grand Duchesses Marie-Adelaide and Charlotte.

Meanwhile, in the Netherlands, though the country had drifted closer to becoming a constitutional monarchy over the nineteenth century, the Dutch monarchy still retained relatively great influence over the government. At ten years old though, Queen Wilhelmina was too young to take an active role in decision-making so her mother, the widowed Queen Emma, acted as regent until Queen Wilhelmina turned 18. Upon becoming old enough to be an active monarch in her own right, Queen Wilhelmina found herself in an anti-British atmosphere, as the Dutch observed the UK's controversial conduct in the Boer War at the turn of the twentieth century. Queen Wilhelmina would have been inclined to sympathise with the Boer farmers opposing British troops due to the kinship she felt with them, given their Dutch origins. It is likely any anti-British feelings Queen Wilhelmina had would have only grown stronger when the Netherlands was caught in the middle of the First World War despite her formal neutrality, with Germany on her eastern border and Great Britain to the west just across the North Sea. Blockades enforced by Great Britain and her allies had a detrimental effect on the Netherlands.

As the First World War drew to a close, and mindful of the downfall of several European monarchies at this time (with the bloody end for the Russian royal family foremost in many people's minds), Queen Wilhelmina felt that she could not afford to be complacent. Therefore, whilst before the War she had very rarely been exposed to the public, having spent much of her life hitherto in the presence of either politicians or fellow royals; afterwards she made an extra effort to engage directly with the public. However, whilst this aided her popularity at home, another decision at the end of the War made Queen Wilhelmina a controversial figure abroad. Over the course of the War, Emperor Wilhelm II of Germany had become a widely demonised and hated figure, seen as one of those most personally responsible for the War taking place. Politicians among the victorious allies were therefore keen to make an example of him, in an apparent display of justice. However, when Emperor Wilhelm II was forced to abdicate and was left with very few and unedifying options as to his fate thereafter, Queen Wilhelmina welcomed him to the Netherlands for his exile, as a show of support for a fellow monarch, not to mention a member of her extended family. When the Great Powers called for the former Emperor Wilhelm II's extradition, Queen Wilhelmina stubbornly refused, providing him with exile for the rest of his life.

The onset of the Second World War marked an end to the still significant influence Queen Wilhelmina hitherto exercised in Dutch politics, a shift in power that would never be restored in quite the same way again to the Dutch monarchy. As the War continued, Dutch efforts to remain neutral, as per the First World War, proved difficult, with the Netherlands ultimately overwhelmed by invading forces from Nazi Germany. Any entrenched wariness of Great Britain that lingered in Queen Wilhelmina's mind had to be cast aside as she found herself having little alternative but to accept the offer of exile provided by Britain's King George VI. Queen Wilhelmina would stay in the United Kingdom for much of the War, endeavouring to boost wartime morale from there by making radio broadcasts that the Dutch public would be able to listen to in secret.

Following the War, by now an elderly woman, Queen Wilhelmina increasingly found that her ability to perform her royal duties was hindered by ill health, relying on her only child, Princess Juliana, to act as regent in her stead. This was at a time when the Netherlands, like much of Europe, was struggling to recover from wartime devastation, as well as confronting the pressures of decolonisation, with the Dutch East Indies fighting for independence, soon resulting in the establishment of the Republic of Indonesia. In 1948, feeling unable to devote herself as actively to her duties as she felt she should at a time of such great challenges, Queen Wilhelmina abdicated, making way for her daughter to succeed her as Queen Juliana. However, despite the formerly pressing concerns about her health, the former Queen Wilhelmina managed to live for over ten years after her abdication, passing away in 1962. In her remaining years, Wilhelmina had nevertheless taken a backseat in national affairs, setting a precedent that both Queen Juliana and then Queen Beatrix, Queen Juliana's eldest daughter and successor, would follow. These three Dutch queens all abdicated in their later years to make way for the next generation. This relatively relaxed attitude towards abdication stood in stark contrast to the British stance, where abdication has been unfavourably associated with the controversial King Edward VIII. Nevertheless, in recent times other European monarchs have likewise chosen to abdicate without the drama of the British abdication in 1936. In fact, from 2013 to 2014, not only Queen Beatrix of the Netherlands but also her counterparts in Belgium, the Vatican City and Spain all abdicated. Incidentally, Queen Beatrix's son and successor, King Willem-Alexander, would be the Netherlands' first king in well over 100 years.

Nicholas

To mark the 1894 accession of Russia's new tsar, Nicholas II, a great feast which the public were invited to was organised; an event that would come to be seen as an omen for the new monarch's reign. Taking place on Khodynka field in Moscow, the celebration turned to tragedy as concern that the food was running out prompted a stampede of people, one that crushed thousands of people to death. A decade later, further potential occasions for celebration took a turn for the worse for Tsar Nicholas II. In the midst of the Russo-Japanese War, after having fathered four daughters, Tsar Nicholas II at last had a son, Tsarevich Alexei, with the Tsar believing that a son would provide Russia with a more suitable and stable heir than a daughter. However, to their great dismay, Tsar Nicholas II and his wife, Empress Alexandra, soon discovered that Tsarevich Alexei had haemophilia, a condition passed down the generations amongst a number of Queen Victoria of Great Britain's descendants, with Empress Alexandra being one of her granddaughters. Haemophilia is a condition that prevents blood from clotting as it naturally would in the event of a wound, meaning that even a minor cut could have fatal consequences for young Alexei, causing great anxiety for his parents.

Moreover, the Russo-Japanese War, lasting from 1904 to 1905, was expected to provide a morale-boosting victory for the Russian Empire. Russia was considered to be one of Europe's Great Powers and, having played a dominant role in world affairs since the end of the early modern era, these countries took for granted that they would always remain in a league above other, non-European powers. The new twentieth century would turn many of these expectations upside-down however, as signalled by the United States of America's victory over Spain in the Spanish-American War at the turn of the century, and Great Britain's struggle to overcome the Boers in South Africa's Boer War around the same time. But the Russo-Japanese War would perhaps be the greatest indicator of a shift in global power, as the long-established Russian Empire was humiliatingly defeated by the rising Japanese Empire. This outcome was not expected of one of Europe's Great Powers, and consequently triggered a deterioration of confidence in Russia's rulers. One such demonstration of this was a peaceful protest by members of the public, who marched on the Tsar's palace in St Petersburg. They were advocates of reform rather than revolution, and even carried portraits of Tsar Nicholas II as signs of respect and loyalty to their ruler, with tsars historically portrayed as father figures for the Russian nation. To their surprise, the demonstrators were fired upon by royal troops, resulting in many deaths. This event, to be known as Bloody Sunday, changed many perceptions of the Russian royal family, creating more sympathy for radical change and revolution. To placate this hostile public mood, the Tsar was compelled to resume the plans of his grandfather, Tsar Alexander II, to install a national parliament. Given his ultra conservative principles, it was with great reluctance that Tsar Nicholas II promptly created the Duma, which duly calmed the public mood.

Tsar Nicholas II never warmed to this new institution, and relentlessly attempted to undermine its authority, changing the voting criteria to empower a richer electorate that he deemed to be more sympathetic to his regime and less likely to make radical demands. Nevertheless, Russia's ruling elite hoped that the 1905 defeat and Bloody Sunday would be the low point of Tsar Nicholas II's reign, and things would only get better. And in the years to follow Russia did appear to stabilise, and the royal family also looked forward to 1913: the year which would mark 300 years of rule in Russia by Tsar Nicholas II's House of Romanov. Though these celebrations were successful, a year later Tsar Nicholas II's Russia would be faced with the fresh and tremendous challenge of the First World War. Whilst wars could often be seen as opportunities to sweep other political issues under the rug, and replace any political divisions with national pride and unity, far-reaching conflicts like the First World War tended to make or break regimes. This would therefore be the greatest test for the Tsarist regime.

Entering the War on the side of Great Britain and France, due to geography Russia nevertheless found herself largely fighting alone on the conflict's Eastern front against combined German and Austro-Hungarian armies. Reminiscent of the Russo-Japanese War a decade earlier, the Russian Empire seemed to struggle once again, with the German and Austro-Hungarian alliance, known as the Central Powers, making great progress into Russian territory, despite the massive size of Russia's armies. To try and turn the tide of the War, Tsar Nicholas II took the drastic step of dismissing the head of the armed forces, the Commander-in-Chief, and adopting the position for himself. This decision would make him the focal point for both praise and criticism of the war effort, depending on the outcome of the conflict. Unfortunately, Tsar Nicholas II did not prove to be a better Commander-in-Chief, while his new role and responsibilities prompted him to delegate much decision-making to Empress Alexandra. Already a controversial figure at this time due to her German heritage, Empress Alexandra attracted even more public scorn and suspicion by her reliance on the mysterious and controversial faith healer, Rasputin, who would wield great influence over her with his extensive advice and apparently divine wisdom. Moreover, Rasputin had gained the ear of the Empress by persuading her that he was one of the few who could genuinely help Tsarevich Alexei overcome the challenges of haemophilia. The apparent infighting among Russia's leaders, demonstrated by the capture and murder of Rasputin by Russian aristocrats in the middle of the War, further discredited the ruling elite's ability to control the country.

In February 1917 discontent with the failing war effort, and the struggle to provide basic supplies both at home and on the battlefront, brought revolution to Russia. This time, the Tsar was advised that only his abdication could save Russia's imperial regime. Tsar Nicholas II complied, but was concerned by who would succeed him: his heir was his son, Tsarevich Alexei, but as a child (and a vulnerable one at that), he was deemed to be an inappropriate successor during these exceptionally difficult times. As such, Tsar Nicholas II looked to his brother, Grand Duke Michael, to succeed him instead, but, given the instability of the country and her monarchy, Grand Duke Michael was reluctant to accept, thus leaving the Russian throne vacant.

Responsibility for governance and the war effort was entirely ceded to a provisional government but, as the year wore on, military success was still not forthcoming. In October 1917, a second revolution brought to power a group of revolutionaries led by Vladimir Lenin, known as the Bolsheviks, who intended to abolish Russia's imperial regime altogether and implement a completely new system of government guided by the ideology of communism, inspired by the nineteenth century works of the political thinker, Karl Marx. The concept was for a new government to rule in the interests of the working class and overturn the traditional dominance of the wealthy and aristocratic classes, with a powerful government enforcing this new system. As the embodiment of the old regime that the Bolsheviks were so opposed to, Tsar Nicholas II and the Russian royal family were imprisoned, and ultimately relocated to Yekaterinburg, where they were placed under house arrest. There were rumours of missions to rescue the Russian royals, spurring on Bolshevik leaders to pre-empt any such rescue attempt. And so one day in 1918, in their Yekaterinburg residence, the Russian royals were led down to the basement, where the former Tsar Nicholas II, Empress Alexandra, all of their children and their accompanying staff, were gunned down. Numerous other members of the Romanov dynasty, including Grand Duke Michael, would also be tracked down and executed.

The Bolsheviks' control of Russia, and what would become their Union of Soviet Socialist Republics, also known as the USSR or Soviet Union, would be tested hot on the heels of the First World War by the Russian Civil War. The Civil War pitted the Bolsheviks' radical left-wing supporters, known as the Reds, against their miscellany of opponents, including international anti-communists and conservative monarchists who could come to rally around Tsar Nicholas II's cousin, Grand Duke Cyril, as the next potential Tsar, in a loose alliance known as the Whites. The Reds were victorious, and the Soviet Union would endure for decades, through the Second World War and Cold War, until its downfall in the early 1990s.

When the Soviet Union was dissolved, there was speculation as to how much the new Russia should look back to the former Russian Empire for inspiration. Tsar Nicholas II's Duma was restored and Russia's second city, called Leningrad by the communist regime as a tribute to their first leader, Vladimir Lenin, was renamed St Petersburg. However, the Russia established in the wake of the Soviet Union would be a federal republic that would soon be dominated by the presidency of another Vladimir, this time, Putin, at the turn of the twenty-first century. Although the manner of Russia's controversial President Putin has been compared with the tsars, he has so far stopped short of granting himself any of their royal titles.

Victor Emmanuel

As the popularity of the Italian monarchy deteriorated during the reign of King Umberto I, culminating in his assassination in 1900, it was down to his son, the new King Victor Emmanuel III, to redeem its reputation. The new king would have been more inclined to look back not to his father but instead his grandfather and namesake, King Victor Emmanuel II of Italy, as a role model, as he had brought the country together in 1862 under Piedmont-Sardinia's Savoy dynasty. Although much of what would become modern Italy had been united under King Victor Emmanuel II by this stage, the new kingdom was able to exploit the subsequent German wars of unification by acquiring first the Veneto region from the defeated Austrian Empire, then was able to seize Rome after French troops stationed there to protect the Pope were recalled to fight in the Franco-Prussian War. Whilst this meant that Rome could now become Italy's capital city, as had long been desired, taking the city from the Pope's control made the Papacy an influential enemy of the young Kingdom of Italy. Thus, it was a significant blow to Italy when Pope Pius IX not only excommunicated King Victor Emmanuel II from the Catholic Church, but also refused to recognise the new Italian state as legitimate.

By the time of King Umberto I's accession, when King Victor Emmanuel II died in 1878, the process of Italian unification largely appeared to have been concluded, so Italian politicians now turned their attentions to establishing an overseas empire during King Umberto I's reign. This was a time of great imperial ambition and competition among Europe's powers, with this exemplified by the notorious 'scramble for Africa', resulting in the annexation of almost the whole continent to European empires: a nearly unbroken stretch of British territory reached from the Cape to Cairo, at the northern and southern tips of Africa, and swathes of Western Africa formed part of the French Empire. Even Belgium joined in, with the Congo, a territory several times larger than Belgium, controversially becoming the personal property of the country's King Leopold II. Meanwhile Italy's imperial efforts generally proved to be disappointing, resulting in the acquisition of only a few African colonies, such as Eritrea and Somalia, whilst King Umberto I's Italy proved embarrassingly unable to defeat and annex Abyssinia (known in the present day as Ethiopia) during the course of their war in the 1890s. It wasn't long after this defeat that King Umberto I's regime was undermined further by the Bava-Beccaris massacre, an infamous incident whereby Italian troops fired upon protestors demonstrating against poor living standards. To add insult to injury, King Umberto I not only expressed support for the troops' actions, but even personally awarded medals to those responsible for firing on the demonstrators. Two years later he was assassinated, and Victor Emmanuel became Italy's miniature monarch (he was 5 feet tall), the man to lead the country into the twentieth century.

King Victor Emmanuel III initially steered clear of controversy by generally avoiding active involvement in government decisions, acknowledging the general trend in Europe towards constitutional monarchy. However, a number of the decisions he later did take would have a major impact on his country. In 1915, with much of Europe plunged into the First World War, Italian politicians were divided as to how their country should become involved, if at all. Before the War, Italy had been linked with Germany and Austria-Hungary in a Triple Alliance. However, this had not compelled Italian involvement at the onset of the War in 1914, and Italians thereafter debated whether to remain neutral or join the Entente Powers of Great Britain, France and Russia. Ultimately, with the enticement of additional territory at the expense of Austria-Hungary if she joined the Entente Powers, King Victor Emmanuel III entered his country into the War on the side of the Entente Powers. This initially appeared to be a good decision, with this being the victorious side, allowing Italy to duly expand her territory as a result, including the annexation of Trieste from the defeated Austro-Hungarian Empire.

In the years following the First World War though, just like many other European countries, regardless of whether they had been on the winning side or not, Italy struggled to recover from the intensity and costs of the conflict, and the instability that resulted. In the early 1920s there still seemed to be no end in sight to these challenges, with Italian governments failing to turn the country's fortunes around. So in 1922, when the fascist Benito Mussolini led a group of his supporters in a march on Rome, King Victor Emmanuel III made another drastic decision for his country: he invited Mussolini to lead an Italian government and become Prime Minister, an invitation which Mussolini duly accepted. It was a controversial step, but King Victor Emmanuel III saw Mussolini as a potentially strong leader who could see Italy through her crisis; one who, despite being a right-wing extremist, would have been deemed by many at the time as a lesser evil when many Europeans (particularly the wealthy) were more fearful of the spread of communism from Russia. This movement had achieved greater credibility thanks to the communists' victory in the Russian Civil War, and appealed to some of the poor and intellectuals during these difficult times as a new alternative. Moreover, for a time, Mussolini was credited with making Italy more stable during the changeable 1920s and 1930s, while international observers saw Mussolini's Italy as a potential bulwark against the expansionist ambitions of Nazi Germany in the early part of the 1930s.

There would be power struggles between Italy's two leaders but, on the one hand, King Victor Emmanuel III gave legitimacy to Mussolini' regime; while on the other, Mussolini seemed to be a stabilising presence in Italy, and some of his decisions would prove to be popular. In the 1920s, decades of tensions between the Kingdom of Italy and the Papacy, which had been a relentless critic of the Italian state from the Pope's residence at the Vatican, were ended by a concordat instigated by Mussolini. This recognised the territory in and around the Vatican as an independent country, the Vatican City, to be ruled by the Pope; whilst Catholicism would officially be Italy's national religion. In exchange, the Italian kingdom would have the Papacy's formal recognition and blessing. Furthermore, in the 1930s Italian armies appeared to redeem themselves after humiliation decades before by finally annexing Abyssinia, with King Victor Emmanuel III also adopting the title of Emperor of Ethiopia.

Though this provided both Mussolini and King Victor Emmanuel III with a prestige boost, the annexation of Abyssinia turned much of the international community against Italy, pushing the country to pursue closer ties with Adolf

Hitler's Nazi Germany. To cultivate this relationship, Mussolini began to pass anti-Jewish legislation, which was in keeping with Nazi Germany's institutionalised anti-Semitism; and all of which sanctioned by King Victor Emmanuel III. With the onset of the Second World War, the fascist Kingdom of Italy was duly allied with Nazi Germany. To begin with, Italy could ride on the coattails of Nazi Germany's swift successes, as more and more territory was promptly added to the sphere of influence of these so-called Axis Powers. It was during these early stages of the War that Italy was able to annex Albania, with King Victor Emmanuel replacing the nation's own King Zog as King of Albania. However, the fortunes of Italy and its leaders were tied to Nazi Germany's success so, when the War went against them, the legitimacy of Mussolini and King Victor Emmanuel III alike plummeted. Anticipating the longer-term impact of this, and the Axis Powers' impending defeat, King Victor Emmanuel III was mindful that, while his own reputation was tied to that of Mussolini's, he believed that the Italian monarchy could at least be saved with some swift action on his part.

In 1944 King Victor Emmanuel III began to pass his duties on to his son and heir, Umberto, and promote him as a budding successor with an untainted reputation. Then in 1946, a year after the War had ended, which had resulted in the defeat and discrediting of Mussolini's regime, King Victor Emmanuel III abdicated in favour of a new King Umberto II. Though, as King Victor Emmanuel III had hoped, his son was a more popular and respected figure than he himself had personally become by the end of the War, this popularity was relative, and the damage to the Italian monarchy's reputation had been too great to ignore. The institution now proved to be very divisive, overwhelmingly so, prompting politicians to hold a referendum on the monarchy a month into King Umberto II's reign. A majority, albeit a narrow one, voted for a republic, forcing the Italian royal family into exile in Egypt, with the former King Victor Emmanuel III dying there a year later, whilst the Italian republic endures to this day.

George

Though the United Kingdom was still in a position of relative strength and stability when he inherited the British throne in 1910, the specific timing of King George V's accession was awkward to say the least. At that time, Great Britain was experiencing a constitutional crisis which, while having seemingly little impact on the public, nevertheless concerned the fundamentals of how the country was governed. Over the centuries, power in Great Britain had gradually shifted from those who held it due to heredity (such as the House of Lords, which formed half of the British parliament, and the monarchy) to those wielding power due to democracy, as symbolised by the other, elected half of the British parliament, the House of Commons. In the build-up to King George V's accession, the elected Liberal government of Herbert Asquith proposed a reformist budget that was passed by the House of Commons, but was blocked by the House of Lords. This stand-off between the elected House of Commons and hereditary and appointed House of Lords would either require the government to compromise on its budget, or the Lords to relent and allow the budget to pass, actions which neither parliamentary chamber were willing to take. Asquith drew in the monarch at the time, the future King George V's father, King Edward VII, and compelled him to agree to flood the House of Lords with Liberal peers to pass the budget if the current composition of the House of Lords refused to relent. Asquith argued that the King needed to back him as a demonstration of support for his democratically-elected government. However, with the death of King

Edward VII, it fell to King George V to agree to Asquith's proposed threat, one which the new king instinctively opposed but pragmatically supported. Consequently, the House of Lords gave in, establishing the precedent of the House of Commons being the superior chamber in the British parliament. The hereditary principle would nevertheless linger on in the House of Lords but, with only half-hearted attempts to reform it since, complete reform of this parliamentary chamber remains outstanding to this day.

Aside from this parliamentary confrontation, the country and institution of monarchy that King George V inherited still enjoyed many of the advantages it had had under both his father, King Edward VII, and his grandmother before him, Queen Victoria. His mother was born a Danish princess, making him first cousin of King Christian X of Denmark. His first cousins also included Emperor Wilhelm II of Germany and Tsar Nicholas II of Russia, placing King George V at the centre of the web of royal family links that extended across Europe. Moreover, the continued strength of the British Empire into the twentieth century appeared to be demonstrated by the Delhi Durbar, the grand ceremony marking the accession of the British monarch as the new Emperor of India, with King George V soon after his accession becoming the first (and last) monarch to personally travel to India to be the focus of this occasion.

These global imperial and royal familial networks that the British royal family sat at the heart of would be seriously threatened and undermined by the First World War. Early on in the conflict, King George V personally tried to stifle tensions between the European powers by writing to his cousins, Emperor Wilhelm II of Germany and Tsar Nicholas II of Russia, in a series of correspondence whereby these royals were addressed informally as Willy and Nicky. However, these royal and family ties failed to make enough of an impact, and soon proved to be first an embarrassment and then a threat to King George V. H.G. Wells, the writer of 'The War of the Worlds', described the King and the British royal family as 'alien and uninspiring'. Upon hearing this, King George V is said to have remarked, "I may be uninspiring, but I'll be damned if I'm an alien!" Nevertheless, this idea of the British royals, supposedly the embodiment of their country, now being deemed a foreign or 'alien' institution, became potentially dangerous for King George V at a time of war. He was a member of the Saxe-Coburg-Gotha dynasty, a German royal house that established itself in Britain thanks to Queen Victoria's marriage to Prince Albert of Saxe-Coburg-Gotha. Whilst this had helped integrate Britain further into

Europe's royal network from the nineteenth century onwards and would aid royal diplomacy, this also resulted in the name of the British royal house being blatantly German at a time when Britain's foremost enemy was the German Empire. Some of the German warplanes attacking the British even had Gotha written on the side of them. King George V was increasingly mindful of these associations of his family with Germany, including the fact that he had many close German relatives, and even his wife, Queen Mary, was German, born with the title Princess of Teck, as a member of the extended royal family of the Kingdom of Wurttemberg, a part of the German Empire. As such, in 1917, to pre-empt questions over the British royals' genuine loyalties, the unconventional step of changing the name of the British royal house was taken to distance the royals from their German roots. After much thought, it was decided that the House of Saxe-Coburg-Gotha in Great Britain should be renamed the House of Windsor, in honour of King George V's favourite royal residence, Windsor Castle.

Another significant act of self-preservation by King George V during the First World War proved to be more ruthless. Hitherto, King George V had enjoyed a good personal relationship with his cousin, Tsar Nicholas II of Russia, with the two even sharing an uncanny likeness to each other. So King George V was understandably concerned when he heard reports of the revolutions in Russia. Loyalty and bonds between European royals had tended to be strong and so, as the situation in Russia deteriorated for the Russian royal family, the British government began to take steps to offer them safe refuge in the United Kingdom. But these steps were abruptly halted by none other than King George V. Despite his personal loyalty and affection for his cousin and his family, King George V was mindful of Tsar Nicholas II's reputation as a bloodstained, autocratic ruler, whose arrival in Britain could be controversial. Consequently, King George V feared that granting the Tsar asylum in Britain could incite resentment towards the royals, maybe even revolution. King George V's instructions to not offer Tsar Nicholas II sanctuary were duly followed, and the Russian royals were left to respond to the revolutionary situation alone, and were ultimately murdered by Bolshevik revolutionaries.

Though the institution of monarchy was greatly shaken in Europe by the First World War, not least by events in Russia, the British monarchy survived and, on the face of it, the British Empire seemed stronger than ever. After the War, the Empire reached its greatest geographical extent, as Britain was able to take territory from the defeated German and Ottoman Empires. Thus, the long-held imperialist ambition of unbroken British territory from Africa's Cape to Cairo was achieved thanks to the acquisition of the German colony, Tanganyika (much of present-day Tanzania), while numerous Middle Eastern colonies were also gained thanks to the Ottomans' final downfall. In practice though, following the War the Empire was also to become more expensive, unwieldy, and increasingly determined to rule itself. At the instigation of Mahatma Gandhi, a successful peaceful opposition to British rule in India gained increasing momentum, while the British government was also left with the awkward responsibility of ruling Palestine, where the rights of the majority Arab Palestinians were weighed against pressure to cultivate the territory as a homeland for Jews, pressure which grew following increased anti-Semitism in Europe encouraged by Adolf Hitler's Nazi regime in Germany. Even the traditionally loyal kindred colonies, with populations largely consisting of British settlers and their descendants, such as New Zealand and Canada, were calling for greater self-government after the War, which was duly accepted in the interwar period by the new concept of self-governing Dominions of the British Empire. Closer to home, King George V oversaw dramatic shifts in the ties between Great Britain and Ireland, which had formally been integrated as one country back in 1801. However there had been limits to the successful integration of the two islands, and relations had been increasingly tense since around the turn of the twentieth century, appearing to reach rock bottom with the Easter Rising of the Irish against British rule during the First World War. King George V closely followed meetings between Irish Nationalists and Unionists, who were in strong opposition and support of union with Great Britain respectively, culminating in a compromise whereby the southern, predominantly Catholic five sixths of Ireland became the Dominion of the Irish Free State, while the remaining northern, largely Protestant counties of Ulster, or Northern Ireland, remained a part of the United Kingdom.

Significant changes also occurred within Great Britain itself, which the traditional and simple King George V, who seemed better suited to the life of a sailor and focusing on his considerable collection of stamps in his free time, appeared remarkably willing to accommodate. The naturally conservative King George V was compelled to appoint Great Britain's first Prime Minister from the left-wing Labour Party, Ramsay MacDonald. The evolution of MacDonald and King George's relationship was drastic. It began with initial mutual suspicion. Then, by the arrival of the 1930s, with the onset of the Great Depression,

MacDonald confessed to the King that he didn't feel up to the job of handling this new crisis. The King disagreed, telling MacDonald that he was the man to form a national government to lead Great Britain through the Depression.

Amidst the great turbulence of his reign, King George V was taken aback and touched by the outpouring of national affection he received during celebrations of his silver jubilee in 1935. Nevertheless, by this point nearing the end of his life, King George V was concerned for the British monarchy following his death. On the face of it, there appeared to be few issues with the line of succession: his son and heir, the Prince of Wales, known as David to the royal family, was a popular figure in Britain and across the Empire and, although childless, the next in line after him was David's younger brother, the less charismatic but nevertheless reliable Bertie who, in turn, had fathered a precocious and seemingly sensible daughter, known affectionately as Lilibet. However, David was unpredictable, had little regard for tradition, and seemed set upon marrying a twice-divorced American, Wallis Simpson. King George V said of his eldest son, "After I am dead, the boy will ruin himself within 12 months," with the old king hoping "that nothing will come between Bertie and Lilibet and the throne". When the life of King George V moved "peacefully towards its close" (the description used in the press as he died) in 1936, the late monarch's opinions of his family proved to be remarkably prophetic. David succeeded his father as King Edward VIII, but was compelled by the ruling elite to abdicate rather than make Wallis Britain's queen, with King Edward duly abdicating only months into his reign. He was succeeded by the steady Bertie who, as King George VI, despite suffering from a debilitating speech impediment, saw his country through the Second World War and the beginning of the end of the British Empire, covering the independence of India and Ireland. At King George VI's premature death in 1952, Lilibet became Queen Elizabeth II, overseeing the independence of virtually the whole of the Empire during her lengthy reign, which became the longest in British history. However, she encouraged former British colonies to retain their historic ties upon independence via the Commonwealth of Nations, an organisation which today has 53 member states, of which 16 still share Queen Elizabeth II as their head of state, including the United Kingdom of Great Britain and Northern Ireland.

Christian

When the newly crowned King Christian X of Denmark inherited the throne from his father, King Frederick VIII, in 1912, he was inheriting one of the oldest monarchies in the world. Having said this, King Christian's dynasty, the House of Glucksburg, was relatively new, having held the Danish throne for barely 50 years by his accession. In 1863, at the death of King Frederick VII of Denmark, the Oldenburg dynasty died with him but, as the House of Oldenburg's extinction had been expected, Prince Christian of Glucksburg, a quite distant relative, had already been groomed as his heir, in part due to his marriage to Princess Louise of Hesse, who was herself a closer relative of the Danish royal family. However, the new King Christian IX of Denmark integrated his Glucksburg dynasty remarkably quickly and deeply into Europe's network of royal families: in addition to fathering the next King of Denmark, the future King Frederick VIII, he was also the father of King George I of Greece, the man selected to replace the young Balkan kingdom's deposed King Otto. Meanwhile, the marriages of two of his daughters to King Edward VII of Great Britain and Tsar Alexander III of Russia meant that, just like King Nikola of Montenegro, King Christian IX of Denmark would be referred to as 'father-in-law of Europe'.

Thus, when his namesake, King Christian X, became King of Denmark, he was inheriting a firmly established throne as part of a well-established dynasty. Nevertheless, while Denmark would be largely unaffected by the First World

War, its hold on its few overseas territories was loosened, with Iceland becoming a self-governing kingdom in its own right at the War's end in 1918, with King Christian X subsequently holding the positions of both Denmark and Iceland's heads of state, keeping the two countries together in a personal union, and becoming the first monarch to hold the title of King of Iceland. Soon after this, King Christian X unexpectedly became embroiled in Danish politics, testing the institution of monarchy in a chain of events known as the Easter Crisis of 1920. At this time, the Danish government was negotiating the future of Schleswig, a region that bordered Germany and had long been a bone of contention between the two countries as to who should control it, and how much of it. The issue proved divisive in Denmark, but the Kingdom's Prime Minister came close to reaching a deal with Germany in terms of how Schleswig should be split; it was at this point that King Christian X felt compelled to break convention and intervene. He dismissed his democratically-elected Prime Minister. Whilst many Danes sympathised with King Christian's stance on Schleswig, his decision to intervene was widely criticised and caused outrage. There were public demonstrations against the King, and King Christian began to deliberate on how he should react to this hostile public response. Soon, King Christian installed a compromise government and new elections were brought forward, in order to bring to power a new government that would undoubtedly reflect public opinion, regardless of the King's preference. The Easter Crisis made the King realise the public's expectations of the monarchy's role, and he would be more cautious with his actions in the future, as would his successors in the future, who would well and truly become constitutional monarchs and remain within the confines of this more restricted role.

King Christian X and the Danish monarchy would survive this crisis, and see the nation through to the Second World War, when Denmark was promptly drawn into the conflict by Nazi Germany's Blitzkrieg tactics, whereby Nazi German armies were able to seize control of many European countries in quick succession, including Denmark. However, whilst many of Europe's royals fled to Great Britain to escape the Nazis, King Christian X did not. During his time in Denmark in the midst of Nazi occupation, the King became a rallying figure for national resistance. At first, the Nazi German leader, Adolf Hitler, attempted to cultivate good relations with King Christian, sending him a warm and lengthy telegram on the occasion of the King's birthday. Being mindful that overt hostility could prove very damaging to himself and his people, King Christian sought subtle ways to rebuke the Nazis instead, so he only implicitly snubbed Hitler's lengthy message by sending a short and curt reply. King Christian's response apparently still made Hitler furious. To boost morale, King Christian X would famously ride on horseback unguarded around the streets of the Danish capital, Copenhagen, as a visible presence of enduring Danish identity for his people. It is also alleged that, during these rides, it was not unknown for the King to be seen wearing an armband bearing the Star of David, the symbol of the Jews, as a sign of solidarity with those who were among the most oppressed by the Nazis.

During this period of wartime occupation, Iceland chose to sever all ties between Iceland and Denmark, making Iceland a completely independent republic in 1944. Thus, King Christian would be both the first and last individual of the modern era to hold the title: King of Iceland. Nevertheless, by the end of the War, King Christian had become an undeniably popular and respected figure, providing national unity for Denmark; marking a complete turnaround from his divisive reputation in the early 1920s. When he died in 1947, King Christian X was succeeded by his son, King Frederick IX, thus prolonging the centuries-old Danish tradition of alternating the names of monarchs from Christian to Frederick. However, a change to Denmark's laws of succession during King Frederick's reign would at least postpone this trend, as he was succeeded by his daughter who still reigns today: Queen Margrethe II.

Karl

The new Emperor Karl inherited the Austro-Hungarian throne from his great-uncle, Emperor Franz Joseph, at an unenviable time: 1916, two years into the First World War. Karl had been heir since his uncle, Archduke Franz Ferdinand, was assassinated in the Bosnian city of Sarajevo in 1914, the assassination triggering the chain of events culminating in the First World War. Although his time as heir was relatively brief, attempts had still been made to prepare Karl for the imperial throne, having served in the military and spent time with Emperor Franz Joseph for some exposure to the monarchy's duties and role in decision-making. Upon inheriting the throne, the young Emperor Karl had clear and apparently laudable aims for his reign.

Firstly, Emperor Karl was keen to bring the War swiftly to an end for his Empire, and felt that a negotiated peace with the opposing Entente Powers would be the most pragmatic means to this. Personally not bearing any grievances towards the Entente Powers, Emperor Karl wanted to tentatively begin peace talks by making use of his contacts within the Entente Powers. Primarily he would rely on his brother-in-law, Prince Sixtus, who, though the son of a Duke of Parma (with the throne of Parma abolished with the unification of the Kingdom of Italy), had close ties with the French establishment. Thus, via Prince Sixtus, Emperor Karl secretly began to send indications of his willingness to negotiate peace separately from his other allies, the German and Ottoman

Empires, who together made up the Central Powers. Consequently, the British, French and Italian governments secretly began to discuss the basis upon which they would be willing to agree peace with the Austro-Hungarian Empire.

Emperor Karl's other goal, which he felt would be best to achieve once the War was over for Austria-Hungary, was to significantly reform the Empire and how its numerous nationalities would be governed. As it was, Emperor Franz Joseph had allowed Hungarians to share the power previously held by the Austrians alone with the Ausgleich compromise of 1867, reforming the Austrian Empire into Austria-Hungary. However, unsurprisingly there were some calls for the other nationalities within the Empire to have greater control over their lands as well, and to not be dominated by either the Austrians or Hungarians. This motivated Archduke Franz Ferdinand, in anticipation of inheriting the Austro-Hungarian throne, to publicly express openness to further reform, whereby the Empire's Slavs could become the third ethnic group to govern the Empire, and thus be on equal terms with the Austrians and Hungarians. The Empire's Slavic people included the Czechs and Slovaks in the north, as well as the Croats and Slovenes to the south, united by speaking similar, Slavic languages. Emperor Karl supported these ideas, and in fact wanted to take them further, advocating self-government for as many of the Empire's ethnic groups as practicable, which would have meant extending self-government to Poles, Italians and Ukrainians as well, among others. The Empire would take on a federal form, whereby each nationality would govern itself to a significant degree, while at the same time an overarching imperial government would be maintained, led by the Emperor. Nationalism had been a powerful force throughout the nineteenth century, breaking the Ottoman Empire in Europe apart into a number of smaller independent nations, whilst elsewhere in the continent nationalism had encouraged the unification of most Germans and Italians under a single empire and kingdom respectively. It was still a powerful political force in the twentieth century, with Emperor Karl hoping, in spite of this trend, to keep his multinational empire together, albeit more loosely, to avoid the alternative he otherwise foresaw, whereby Austria-Hungary would be divided into numerous, smaller nation states.

Unfortunately, whilst Emperor Karl's ambitions for peace and imperial reform may seem reasonable, they would backfire significantly. Over time, Emperor Karl's peace talks seemed to be bearing fruit, with much of the basis for peace terms agreed between Austria-Hungary and the Entente Powers. But a persistent stumbling block was calls from Italy for Austria-Hungary to concede more territory to her than Emperor Karl was willing to agree to, which ultimately brought the negotiations to an unsuccessful end. And worse was to come. Following the end of these talks, word of these secret negotiations spread and eventually became public, with national leaders engaging in confusing and very public squabbles over these negotiations. Confusion emerged as those involved in talks gave conflicting versions of events, with some sharing the truth, while others attempted to tell lies or deny that they had even happened. Eventually, all parties publicly accepted that the talks did indeed take place, leading to Austria-Hungary's key ally, Germany, becoming amongst those most furious that Austria-Hungary had tried to negotiate withdrawal from the War behind their back. Many of Emperor Karl's own subjects also felt betrayed: they saw it that they were going through the hardships of wartime, and putting their lives on the line, for a cause that their own emperor clearly didn't believe in. Emperor Karl was no longer trusted by Germany's ruling elite, with Emperor Wilhelm II adding to pressure for Austro-Hungarian forces to be more closely integrated with those of Germany in response and play a more subordinate role in the war effort. These developments had a detrimental effect on Emperor Karl's reputation among the Entente Powers too: he had gone from a sympathetic opponent that they could do business with, to Emperor Wilhelm II's puppet, with the Entente Powers consequently now less concerned with the fate of Emperor Karl and the Habsburg Empire.

If anything, as the War continued into 1918, pressure mounted on the Entente Powers to consider dismantling the Austro-Hungarian Empire in the event of their increasingly-likely victory. Since entering the War in 1917, the United States of America's influence would grow in terms of both the Entente war effort and the post war settlement, thanks to her significant contribution and resources. One of the USA's stated war aims was to support self-government for nations, implicitly attacking the idea of multinational empires like Austria-Hungary. Thus, with Emperor Karl discredited by the failed peace talks, referred to as the Sixtus Affair, the USA and her European allies were increasingly inclined to support emerging nationalist leaders who promoted the idea of newly independent countries, such as Czechoslovakia, to be established at Austria-Hungary's expense.

With the War drawing to a close, Emperor Karl made a last-ditch attempt to realise his goal of a federal empire, and avoid the dissolution of his country, by bringing forward his plans to devolve power to the Empire's nations, even though the War was still being fought. It was his hope that enacting these plans would endear him more to his subjects of all nationalities. At the same time, Emperor Karl believed this would win over the Entente Powers to the idea of preserving the Habsburg Empire because self-government was now being conceded to Austria-Hungary's different nationalities, in accordance with the widely-stated aims of the Entente Powers. But again, Emperor Karl's actions worked against him: rather than holding the Empire together, implementing these reforms during a time of instability and impending defeat instead hastened its dissolution, with nationalist politicians exploiting these new devolved powers and using them to ultimately achieve national independence.

At the end of the War, Emperor Karl saw his power and territory swiftly dwindle due to Austria-Hungary's defeat. Remaining in Schonbrunn Palace in the Austro-Hungarian capital, Vienna, Emperor Karl was informed that, in the north, Czechoslovakia was breaking away to form an independent republic, while the Croats and Slovenes were integrating with their fellow south Slavs in Serbia to form what would ultimately become the Kingdom of Yugoslavia. Closer to home, Hungary was in turmoil, going through a range of governmental systems in quick succession. Meanwhile in Austria, politicians decided upon forming a republic, thus deposing Karl as Emperor. Pressure was put on Karl to abdicate to formalise these changes, but he refused to do so. Karl therefore would remain uneasily in his palace in this tenuous position until he was forced out of Austria and into exile in Switzerland. He would be transported there by a British armed escort at the instigation of King George V, perhaps to ensure that Austria's Habsburgs didn't meet the same fate as Russia's Romanovs. Hot on the heels of Karl's departure, in 1919 the Austrian government passed a law banning Karl and members of his Habsburg dynasty from entering their country unless the Habsburg concerned pledged their allegiance to the new Austrian republic.

In his Swiss exile, the former Emperor Karl was restless; he was keen to retake his imperial throne, which he saw as still legitimately his, given that he had never agreed to abdicate. In reality however the former Habsburg lands were consolidating their new borders and governments, with seemingly little chance of Karl being restored as monarch. Most seemed increasingly successful in this endeavour, but Hungary appeared to be an exception. Having tried one system of government after another, including a republic and even a communist government, the nation settled on becoming a kingdom. What remained unsettled was who would be Hungary's king. Though the obvious candidate, Karl's wartime conduct and international reputation made him too controversial a choice at this time. Other members of the Habsburg dynasty were considered but, for the time being, a regent was to be selected. This position would be filled by Miklos Horthy, a conservative figure who was a widely respected war veteran, having served as an admiral in the Austro-Hungarian navy in the First World War.

By 1921, Karl felt that a conservative Kingdom of Hungary led by Horthy, a kindred spirit in Karl's eyes, would now welcome him back as King. Therefore, in secret, Karl decided to travel to Hungary. Surprising Horthy, Karl had tracked him down and thanked the Regent for his service, but said that he was now ready to retake the Hungarian throne for himself. Karl did not receive the warm welcome he expected, with Horthy refusing to concede the Hungarian throne back to Karl, saying that his restoration would undermine the nation's greater stability and recovery since the War, and would antagonise neighbouring countries that had grown at the expense of the Habsburgs and their former empire. It is true that lingering sympathy for the Habsburgs among their former subjects was a concern for the leaders of those countries that had been established, or had expanded their territory, thanks to the dissolution of Austria-Hungary. National leaders in Central Eastern Europe therefore feared a Habsburg restoration would undermine them by dividing the loyalties of their people, and they were also concerned that Karl would attempt to redraw national borders again, this time at *their* expense.

Whether Horthy's refusal to support Karl was primarily down to Horthy's pragmatic concerns for his country, or simply his own ambitions to remain Hungary's head of state, is open to debate, but whatever Horthy's main motivation was, Karl's failure to get Horthy's backing led to the former emperor returning to Switzerland. But not for long. Within months, Karl would go back to Hungary and attempt to retake the throne again. This time, knowing he lacked Horthy's support, Karl would instead seek the support of sympathetic politicians and aristocrats, and encourage an uprising against Horthy's regime. Travelling back to Hungary by aeroplane, a novel means of transport at the time, Karl successfully rallied a small army of supporters, but so did Horthy. The two sides clashed, with Karl and Horthy's armies fighting for control of Hungary. However, when it became clear that no side would achieve a swift victory, Karl withdrew his forces. This time, he would not be permitted to quietly return to

Switzerland. He was now deemed a threat to the stability of the continent, with the European powers agreeing that Karl should be sent to a more remote and distant exile, reminiscent of the former Emperor Napoleon I of France just over a century earlier. Although both former emperors were ultimately sent to islands in the Atlantic Ocean, whilst Napoleon had been exiled to British-held St Helena, Karl would be escorted to the Portuguese territory of Madeira. Karl's exile there would be brief as his health soon deteriorated, dying prematurely in 1922, aged only 34.

Vasyl

Over the course of the First World War, the relationship between Archduke Karl Stefan of Austria and his youngest son, Archduke Wilhelm, proved to be very changeable. Initially, it seemed as though Archduke Wilhelm's ideals would undermine Archduke Karl Stefan's carefully prepared plans for his family; towards the end of the War though, these same ideals seemed likely to consolidate the position of Archduke Karl Stefan and his branch of the extensive Habsburg dynasty. For, over the course of 1917 and into 1918, there was a significant opportunity for Archduke Karl Stefan to be crowned King of Poland, while Archduke Wilhelm, known with affection as Prince Vasyl by his Ukrainian supporters, could have become King of Ukraine.

For a long time beforehand, Archduke Karl Stefan had been discreetly laying the foundations for his branch of Austria's old dynasty to become Poland's new royal family. Archduke Karl Stefan had been brought up in a traditional royal household, but he had also lived through a time of tremendous change in Europe, as nationalist forces transformed the continent around Austria-Hungary that had been established by the conservative Great Powers at the Congress of Vienna. In the Europe Archduke Karl Stefan had grown up in, national identity was increasingly replacing dynastic power politics and empire-building as the basis for a country. More countries were being established based on a shared language and culture, with the elephant in the room being the multinational Austro-

Hungarian Empire of the Habsburgs at the heart of Europe. Archduke Karl Stefan anticipated that Austria-Hungary would not remain immune to this trend, and perhaps only the elderly Emperor Franz Joseph held the country together after all these years. But the old emperor wouldn't be around forever, so Archduke Karl Stefan began to prepare himself and his family for the day that change finally reached the Austro-Hungarian Empire. Thus, Archduke Karl Stefan established his family home in a castle in Poland, and ensured that his children could speak Polish and had a strong understanding of the nation's history and culture. He also cultivated close ties between his family and the Polish nobility and, in time, Archduke Karl Stefan would encourage his daughters to marry Polish noblemen.

For much of Archduke Karl Stefan's life, Poland had not existed as an independent country. It had done so throughout much of the early modern period, and in fact during that time had been an influential European power. However, what had been the Polish-Lithuanian Commonwealth saw its fortunes transformed, and was dismembered towards the end of the early modern era; the Polish lands were divided between what was at the time the Habsburgs' Holy Roman Empire, the Russian Empire and the Kingdom of Prussia. Although Poland as a country had therefore been largely eradicated, memories of it had not, and many Poles hoped for the restoration of their independence; a cause they rose up for in 1830 during that time of European instability. However, whilst many Europeans sympathised with the Poles, as the former Polish nation was now engulfed by powerful, conservative empires, there was little that their supporters elsewhere on the continent would be willing or able to do to help. Nevertheless, as time wore on, it became harder to ignore the various causes for national independence across Europe and, when that movement penetrated Austria-Hungary, Archduke Karl Stefan hoped he had successfully positioned himself as the obvious candidate, should there be a vacancy, for a King of Poland.

Whilst Archduke Karl Stefan's family largely followed his lead with positioning themselves as a prospective Polish royal family, there was one member who clearly took an alternative stance: his youngest son, Archduke Wilhelm. With age, instead of taking an interest in Polish culture as encouraged by his father, Archduke Wilhelm grew increasingly curious about the Ukrainian nation instead. This came to be a concern because, where the lands of the Poles and Ukrainians overlapped, Archduke Wilhelm made clear that his sympathies were with the Ukrainians, which was in complete defiance of his father's wishes.

With the onset of the First World War, Archduke Wilhelm enthusiastically played a leading role among Austria-Hungary's Ukrainian troops. His respect for their culture endeared him to his troops, who gave him the nickname Vasyl Vyshyvani: Ukrainian for Basil the Embroidered, in homage to their flamboyant royal sponsor. Archduke Wilhelm's status as a military leader among the Ukrainians seemed set to become a political one too thanks to further developments in the War. Following the Russian revolutions of 1917, the new Bolshevik government in Russia became determined to pull their country out of the War, seemingly at any cost, in order to give them the chance to implement their communist ideology as soon as possible. As a consequence, in the spring of 1918, the Treaty of Brest-Litovsk was signed between Russia's Bolshevik government and the Central Powers. This would end conflict between the signatories. In exchange, the Russian government would concede whole swathes of its European territory to the German and Austro-Hungarian Empires. When the two powers sought to share this new territory, it seemed as though it would be split on a basis whereby the northern territories would come under German influence, whilst the central lands would be incorporated within the Habsburg sphere. Under this arrangement, the Polish and Ukrainian territory hitherto held by the Russian Empire would now come under the Habsburgs. In keeping with his ambitions to devolve more power to the numerous nations which came under his rule, Emperor Karl of Austria-Hungary appeared willing to concede the Austro-Hungarian lands where Poles and Ukrainians were a majority to the prospective newly independent countries of Poland and Ukraine. These plans also included potentially making these new countries kingdoms, with Archduke Karl Stefan to be King of Poland and Archduke Wilhelm King of Ukraine, thus making these countries part of a broader Habsburg sphere that would have a more extensive reach over Central and Eastern Europe.

These plans were soon undermined when Archduke Wilhelm, despite his enthusiasm for Ukraine and his bond with the Ukrainian people, was increasingly side-lined thanks to German influence, with the German Empire more enthusiastic about Petro Skoropadsky, a pro-German from an influential Ukrainian family, becoming the Hetman, effectively dictator, of the newly independent Ukraine. As the months passed, the plans of both Archduke Karl Stefan and Archduke Wilhelm would be scuppered by Austria-Hungary's defeat in the First World War. Unsurprisingly, the Entente Powers were unlikely to support new nations being led by old enemies, so Poland and Ukraine became republics instead. Whilst Archduke Karl Stefan's dreams ended there, his idealistic son was less willing to accept defeat.

Wilhelm upheld his Ukrainian connections and, for the time being at least, was willing to make his hopes to become the nation's monarch a secondary priority to the retention of Ukraine's newly-won independence. Hence why, at the turn of the 1920s, Wilhelm backed Ukraine's ultimately unsuccessful campaigns in wars with neighbouring Poland and the Soviet Union. In the face of defeat, and disillusioned with the Ukrainian government's handling of these wars, an embittered Wilhelm left the country, resentful towards both the Ukrainian government and the Soviet Union's growing influence in Eastern Europe. He would settle in Paris, France, where he put his political ambitions on ice and, for a time, indulged in more decadent passions; sharing many romantic encounters with women and men alike, usually wearing a shirt and trousers, but occasionally while wearing a dress. By the mid-1930s, Wilhelm's scandalous lifestyle got out of hand, with an impending messy court case that would expose dirty money and his complex love life, prompting him to abscond to Austria.

At this time, the extreme right-wing ideology of Adolf Hitler was penetrating more and more deeply into first Germany and then elsewhere in Europe, with Austria, Hitler's country of birth, set in his sights for annexation to a Nazi German Empire. Though widely despised during and after the Second World War, Hitler and his ideology were tolerated, and even supported, by many before the War as a strong alternative to what was then seen as a greater threat by many in Europe's elite: communism, as spawned by the Soviet Union. Wilhelm's aristocratic connections in Central Europe, coupled with his long-held hatred of the Soviet Union, led him into pro-Nazi social circles during his period in Austria. For a time, Wilhelm, with the encouragement of those he now spent his time with, wondered whether Nazi Germany was not only a lesser evil to the Soviet Union, but if its conquest and transformation of Europe could even present the opportunity for a Kingdom of Ukraine, free from Soviet influence, with himself as its king at last. However, as the Second World War progressed, it became increasingly clear to Wilhelm that his hopes were unlikely to materialise, and ultimately wanted to distance himself from the Axis Powers' ambitions in Europe. In fact, Wilhelm drew closer to his contacts in Great Britain during the course of the War, and became a spy for Britain against the Nazis.

Following the War Wilhelm continued to act as a spy, in collaboration with Great Britain and France; but he would shift his target for intelligence-seeking from Germany towards the Soviet Union, reflecting the emerging Cold War tensions that were manifesting themselves in post war Europe. However, in 1947 Wilhelm's secret role was uncovered by Soviet spies, who captured and imprisoned him. In the year that followed, he died in a Soviet prison from untreated tuberculosis.

Mindaugas

Although a candidate for numerous thrones, the greatest of these opportunities for Wilhelm, Duke of Urach, to at last become a head of state appeared to arrive in 1918, when he began to be recognised as King Mindaugas II of Lithuania. Wilhelm had interesting origins: he was a royal with good connections, yet he was not the direct heir to a particular throne. He was born the son of the Duke of Urach, a junior member of the royal family of the German Kingdom of Wurttemberg, which was itself part of the German Empire. However, despite these strong German roots, and inheriting the German title of Duke of Urach, he was also closely tied with Monaco as a consequence of his mother being the sister of Prince Charles III of Monaco.

Though Wilhelm already held the title of Duke of Urach, it was only with the arrival of the twentieth century that the opportunities to become a head of state began to materialise: in fact, he would be in line for three such positions, each with varying chances of success, over the course of a decade. The first came just before the First World War, when the traditional royal order still appeared to be as firmly in place as it had been over the preceding century. Consequently, it was still the assumption that, whenever a country newly became independent, it would become a monarchy, with a member of an established royal family (often from a minor German dynasty) usually appointed as head of state of the new country. This was to be the case when, as a consequence of the Balkan Wars, whereby the declining Ottoman Empire fought against its former territories (now independent states) found in the Balkan region, much of the remaining Ottoman territory in Europe was thereafter to be recognised as the independent Principality of Albania. Europe's Great Powers began to consider a number of candidates to become the first Prince of Albania. Given his connections, and coinciding with the fact that he was not deemed likely to inherit another throne, Wilhelm of Urach was one of those considered most favourably to take this position. However, another minor German royal, Prince William of Wied, was selected instead, having received enthusiastic backing to take the new Albanian throne from his aunt, who had through marriage become the Queen of Romania.

Although Wilhelm missed the Albanian opportunity, more seemed likely to arise towards the end of the War. In early 1918, while on the one hand the Entente Powers were severely weakened by the loss of their Russian ally due to the Russian revolutions, their fortunes were nevertheless expected to swiftly improve as the United States of America was to set to join their military campaign. The Central Powers therefore hoped to overwhelm the Entente alliance and win the War before the benefit of American support could make an impact. The shape of how Europe would look in the event of a victory for the Central Powers was indicated by the outcome of the Treaty of Brest-Litovsk, signed by the leading Central Powers, Germany and Austria-Hungary, with the new communist Russian government who were keen to withdraw their country from the War as soon as possible. This treaty ceded significant territory to the Central Powers, which they intended to set up as numerous independent, but allied, states. In keeping with the convention of new countries being established as monarchies, a number of minor royals now had the chance to claim these countries for themselves. Prince Frederick Charles, a member of the no-longer reigning German House of Hesse, was lined up as King of Finland, able to exploit the advantage given to him of being brother-in-law to Emperor Wilhelm II of Germany. Meanwhile, some of the territory acquired along the coast of the Baltic Sea was to become the United Baltic Duchy, an outpost of the German Empire, with Adolf Friedrich, a member of the minor German House of Mecklenburg, put forward to be its duke.

Another part of the Baltic region was set aside to become the independent Kingdom of Lithuania: this would allow Wilhelm of Urach to once again enter the frame to become a national leader. Wilhelm's German connections stood him in good stead when it came to the Central Powers choosing a friendly royal to place on the prospective Lithuanian throne. As such, representatives of the Central Powers and Lithuanian politicians invited Wilhelm to become King of Lithuania, an offer he accepted. In recognition of Lithuania's past as an independent kingdom in medieval times, Wilhelm expressed his intention to adopt the name of a former Lithuanian monarch, Mindaugas, and consequently accede as King Mindaugas II of Lithuania. Wilhelm's chances of becoming king were to fall as swiftly as they had risen though, as his prospects were linked to Germany's fortunes in the War. When German defeat became inevitable, the offer of the Lithuanian throne was withdrawn from Wilhelm. Lithuania became a republic at the end of the War, as did Finland, while the intended United Baltic Duchy was instead split into the two republics of Estonia and Latvia.

Wilhelm had now lost out on two chances to become a monarch, but one distant prospect still lingered. Thanks to his connections to Monaco's royal family, as the grandson of Prince Florestan I of Monaco, he was in the line of succession to their throne. What needs to be taken into consideration though is that the tiny Principality of Monaco was surrounded by France, and the locations and sizes of Monaco and France made the former very dependent on the latter. As such, given that France and Germany were bitter wartime enemies during the First World War, Monaco's dominant French neighbour was unlikely to welcome the prospect of a German like Wilhelm becoming Monaco's head of state. Meanwhile the fact that, in the early twentieth century, Prince Albert I of Monaco's son and heir, Louis, looked increasingly unlikely to father any legitimate offspring, meant Wilhelm's chances of one day becoming Prince of Monaco seemed to grow as time wore on. With the French government hostile towards this prospect, and Monegasque leaders keen to remain on good terms with France, steps were pre-emptively taken to make Wilhelm's eventual accession less likely. As tensions between France and Germany were growing in the build-up to the War, Louis' illegitimate daughter, Charlotte, was legitimised, thus pushing Wilhelm further down the line of succession.

Wilhelm's chances of becoming Prince of Monaco were virtually wiped out by the signing of a treaty in 1918 between France and Monaco, stipulating that all Princes of Monaco thereafter needed to be either French or Monegasque citizens, and needed the approval of the French government. Furthermore, in the event of the Monegasque throne becoming vacant, the treaty allowed for Monaco to become a French territory (an eventuality only overturned by a further treaty between the two countries signed in 2002, which safeguarded Monaco's independence regardless of the Principality's line of succession). Nevertheless, in 1922, when Prince Albert I died and was succeeded by Louis II, with Charlotte now heir, Wilhelm renounced his place in Monaco's line of succession, despite him being somewhat unlikely to inherit the throne in any case. So in 1928, with the German Empire long gone, Wilhelm consequently died only as the duke of the defunct duchy of Urach.

Otto

Despite still being a relatively young man at his death, the former emperor Karl of Austria-Hungary had at least managed to father a number of offspring who could continue his claim to the former Habsburg realms, with Crown Prince Otto the eldest of his eight children, and therefore the heir to his claim upon his death in 1922. With the former emperor now having passed away, sympathisers with the former Austro-Hungarian royal family felt that the European powers would be less hostile to the prospect of them returning to the continent from their exile on Madeira. Therefore, at the instigation of King Alfonso XIII of Spain, himself the son of an Austrian archduchess, the former Empress Zita of Austria-Hungary and her children were able to relocate to Spain.

In any case, with the onset of the 1930s, the Habsburgs were likely to be amongst the least of European leaders' concerns, given the rise of Adolf Hitler, who was consolidating his control of Germany as Fuhrer, spouting hostile rhetoric and flouting the restrictions imposed on Germany by the Treaty of Versailles, the peace agreement signed at the end of the First World War. Austria seemed to be one of Hitler's main targets when it came to his ambitions to expand Germany's borders and influence, seeing as the two countries neighboured each other and shared German as their national language. Initially, the threat posed by Hitler to Austrian independence seemed less great due to the international support Austrian leaders expected in the event of a potential invasion, notably from neighbouring Italy, led by the strongman Benito Mussolini. However, with the passage of time, Mussolini became one of Hitler's closest allies, whilst two of Europe's Great Powers at this time, Great Britain and France, which were previously counted upon to keep the peace on the continent, now seemed far less reliable. This was due to their policy of appeasing Hitler, whereby they hoped that, if enough was conceded to Hitler, he would be satisfied and no longer threaten the status quo in Europe. As such, a number of Austrians, including the Chancellor of the Republic of Austria, Kurt Schuschnigg, feared that the annexation of Austria by Nazi Germany was a concession Great Britain and France would be willing to accept. Moreover, such an annexation, known as Anschluss, was a prospect welcomed by many Austrians who advocated union with their powerful neighbour, with whom they felt they had much in common.

Nevertheless, there were also many Austrians who strongly opposed Anschluss and wanted independence preserved; not least Austrian Jews, who feared that the anti-Semitic measures in place in Nazi Germany would be extended to Austria were Anschluss to take place. At the time, the Habsburgs and their former empire were still associated with Austria's national identity and what made the country distinctive. As such, with the likelihood of Anschluss growing in the mid-1930s, Kurt Schuschnigg began secret discussions with Otto von Habsburg (as the Habsburg heir was usually known as following Austria-Hungary's dissolution) about the potential restoration of the Austrian monarchy. Otto was keen to be installed as Austria's monarch and, now a young adult, had the popular backing in this endeavour from a number of Austrians who saw him as a potential bulwark against Nazi expansionism. However, Otto and Schuschnigg were too slow with their talks to achieve any tangible progress before Anschluss took place in 1938, prompting the deposition of Schuschnigg and his imprisonment by invading Nazi German forces.

Otto knew that he would also be a high-profile target, with Nazi plans to invade Austria even known as Operation Otto. As such, during the Second World War Otto made his escape from Europe to the United States of America at the invitation of President Franklin D Roosevelt. On good terms with the Allied Powers, Otto received influential support from British Prime Minister Winston Churchill, who even lobbied the rest of the Big Three Allied Powers (i.e., the United States and Soviet Union, in addition to Great Britain) to recognise Otto after the War as the leader of a confederation of Central European nations, consisting of the former territories of the Austro-Hungarian Empire. However, as the War drew to an end, the Soviet Union was coming to be recognised as a superpower and had firmly established military dominance over Eastern Europe, including much of the former territory of the Habsburgs. As such, the replacement of Soviet influence in the region with a Western-allied Habsburg confederation was very unlikely to materialise following the Second World War. Indeed, with Austria the primary exception, the former Habsburg lands had communist governments imposed on them by the Soviet Union at the end of the War. The divide between the Central-Eastern European countries under communist rule and those with capitalist regimes to the west marked what Churchill would famously describe as the Iron Curtain. This separation of the hostile capitalist and communist states of Europe from each other embodied the Cold War tensions that would continue to be felt across the world for decades to come.

Austria, which was able to preserve a capitalist regime with democratic government after the Second World War, proved to be a less hostile environment for Otto than it had been for his father, Karl, at the end of the First World War. Otto was permitted to return to Austria and had become a popular figure, receiving honorary citizenship from many Austrian towns. There were limits to this gregariousness however, with Otto still forced to pledge allegiance to the Austrian republic before he was allowed to return. Otto obliged, but for purely pragmatic reasons, as he still believed that constitutional monarchy would be the best system of government for Austria. Though coming to appreciate that he was now unlikely to achieve sufficiently influential support to become Austria's monarch, Otto nevertheless maintained a strong interest in government and politics, and sought alternative means to leaving a legacy and making a difference. As well as being an advocate of constitutional monarchy, Otto was a champion of European integration and cooperation; and if this could not be achieved via a modern-day Austro-Hungarian Empire, Otto would instead channel his enthusiasm for this cause towards the growing European Economic Community, or EEC, instead. With the foundations for this embodiment of a united Europe put in place soon after the Second World War, the group of six Western European countries that made up the original membership of the EEC was expanded to nine in the 1970s as Great Britain, Ireland and Denmark also joined. Otto lobbied for the countries that were former Habsburg territories to become members as well, and was able to gain a platform for this campaign once he was elected as one of Germany's Members of European Parliament in 1979.

Otto was by no means the only royal to pursue a political career in a republic. On the one hand there were the older examples of Emperor Napoleon III of the French and King Zog of the Albanians, who used their respective republics as a means to achieving their own monarchical ambitions. But there were also others who, like Otto, would pursue less belligerent political careers in more recent times. Aside from Otto von Habsburg was the other notable case of the former Tsar Simeon II of Bulgaria. In a life that would often mirror that of his contemporary, King Michael of neighbouring Romania, Simeon likewise inherited a Balkan throne as a child. Simeon became Tsar of Bulgaria during the Second World War aged six following the death of his father, Tsar Boris III, who had made his country a wartime ally of Nazi Germany. Tsar Simeon II's family exercised royal duties on his behalf, given how young he was at his accession, with this arrangement continuing throughout the rest of the War and beyond, albeit in an awkward position during these post War years, given the communist government imposed upon on Tsar Simeon and his country by Soviet occupiers. The difficult governmental system in Bulgaria of preserving a monarchy that oversaw a communist dictatorship was soon brought to an end when Simeon and the rest of the Bulgarian royal family were forced into exile after a questionable referendum on the monarchy held in 1946 by the communists.

During the time of Bulgaria's communist regime, Simeon lived the life of a private citizen, much of it in Spain. With the downfall of communism in Europe in the 1990s, Simeon, like a number of his contemporary royals, returned to Eastern Europe, with the former monarch becoming a popular figure among some Bulgarians, spurring a degree of public support for the restoration of the monarchy. But curiously, whereas his royal counterparts elsewhere in Eastern Europe chose to promote the restoration of the monarchy by lobbying politicians and making public appearances, Simeon instead set up his own political party, National Movement Simeon II, and contested elections to become Prime Minister of the Republic of Bulgaria in 2001. He won the election, and Simeon duly became Prime Minister of Bulgaria. Though Simeon had some successes as Prime Minister, notably seeing his country become a member of the NATO military alliance, the royal magic soon wore off during his term of office. Over the next few years Simeon would see his own political fortunes and those of his political party decline, voted out of office in 2005 and thereafter largely drifting out of the public eye. Nevertheless, as it stands, he has achieved more prominence (however short-lived) than any of his Balkan counterparts.

The political career of Otto von Habsburg, meanwhile, would last considerably longer. A decade on from his first election as an MEP, by which point communism's grip on Europe had become considerably weaker, Otto encouraged its further decline and the breakdown of the division between Eastern and Western Europe by helping to organise the Pan-European Picnic, which called upon Europeans on either side of the Iron Curtain to meet at the border between Austria and Hungary. With the downfall of communism in Europe soon after, Otto stepped up his campaign for the Eastern European countries now adopting democracy and capitalism to be made members of what had become the European Union as soon as possible. In 1999 Otto's career as an MEP ended after two decades, with the now 86-year-old royal looking to retire from the various positions he held. Eight years later Otto recognised his eldest son, Karl, as head of the House of Habsburg-Lorraine, and implicitly as claimant to the former Habsburg thrones. In 2011, Otto passed away aged 98. In tribute to Otto, as the final Crown Prince of Austria-Hungary, and prominent European politician and advocate of European integration, he had an extravagant and well-publicised funeral. In keeping with his family's tradition, Otto's body was buried in Austria, while his heart was buried in Hungary. Royals and republican politicians alike attended the funeral and paid tribute to Otto, many of whom coming from the various independent countries that now cover the former lands of the Habsburgs.

Michael

When King Ferdinand died in 1927, he was succeeded as King of Romania not by his son, Prince Carol, but instead by his grandson, who became King Michael of Romania at the age of five. The late King Ferdinand's determination to oppose his country's alignment with the Central Powers during the First World War did wonders for his prestige when the Entente Powers became ultimately victorious. It also resulted in the vast expansion of his country at the expense of the former Austro-Hungarian Empire, due to the cession of Transylvania to Romania. Prince Carol's reputation did not weather as well as that of his father though, as he was compelled to renounce his place in the Romanian line of succession in 1925 because of his ongoing affair with Magda Lupescu, whilst married to Princess Helen of Greece, daughter of King Constantine I of Greece.

And so it was that Michael inherited the Romanian throne. However, too young to reign in his own right, King Michael's uncle Prince Nicolas carried out most of his duties for him as regent. The regency proved to be a difficult time though, with Romania exposed to the instability most European countries experienced following the First World War, and the Romanian royal family was drawn into the murky world of politics. Over time, the disgraced Prince Carol was enticed to return and displace the influence of his brother, Prince Nicolas, and dethrone his own son, King Michael. This culminated in a coup in 1930 that ended the reign of King Michael and Prince Nicolas, making Carol King Carol

II of Romania. His reign saw conflict and competition for power between the conservative, right-wing King Carol II and the even more right-wing, fascist Iron Guard movement, which welcomed the growing influence of Nazi Germany in Europe. By 1940 the influence of both the Iron Guard, led by Ion Antonescu, in Romania, and Nazi Germany's Axis allies in Europe, became overwhelming, with Antonescu establishing a pro-Nazi dictatorship in Romania while King Carol II abdicated and went into exile. Meanwhile Michael, now a young adult, was restored as King of Romania, with Antonescu hoping King Michael could legitimise his regime while, at the same time, the monarch's youth was likely to prevent him from interfering with his dictatorship.

Nevertheless, during the course of the Second World War King Michael developed a mind of his own, in spite of his youth, and found others in the Romanian ruling elite who shared his distaste for their country's alliance with the Axis Powers. Together, in 1944, King Michael and his supporters organised a coup that deposed Ion Antonescu, and Romania's war effort was realigned to support the Allies instead. King Michael's coup earned the monarch popularity at home and respect abroad. As such, while a number of King Michael's fellow monarchs in Eastern Europe were deposed or prevented from returning to their countries due to the rise of communism in the region, whether by home-grown communists or those installed by the rising superpower, the Soviet Union, King Michael was one of the few able to remain. However, Romania's close geographical proximity to the overwhelming Soviet Union meant that her Western-aligned regime would not be tolerated for long. A very uneasy compromise was therefore established, whereby a Soviet-backed communist government was installed in Romania, but King Michael would retain some influence as he stayed on as head of state. King Michael and his communist government did not get on, with the King repeatedly coming to blows with the communists and resisting giving the laws they proposed his royal assent. This difficult state of affairs was prolonged until 1947 when, perhaps inevitably, King Michael was forced to abdicate, apparently at gunpoint, with the threat of widespread bloodshed from the communists and the lives of Romanian students allegedly also threatened if he refused to step down. And so King Michael duly abdicated and went into exile, whilst the communist regime consolidated its control of Romania.

Whilst 1947 had been a difficult year, to say the least, for Michael, it was not *all* bad for him. That year, when attending the wedding of the future Queen

Elizabeth II of Great Britain to Prince Philip of Greece, Michael had the good fortune to meet Princess Anne of the royal house of Parma, which had ruled the by now defunct Italian duchy. A year after meeting, Michael and Anne married, and would settle into exile in Switzerland. Michael monitored Romania from his Swiss exile as the infamous communist dictator, Nicolae Ceaucescu, imposed his brand of communism on Michael's former kingdom for decades. However, in 1989, as communist regimes appeared to be falling like dominoes across Eastern Europe, Ceaucescu attempted to hold on, to his great cost: Ceaucescu was forced from power in December 1989 in a popular revolution, with the dictator and his wife captured and executed, with their corpses publicly displayed on Christmas Day. As democracy began to emerge across Eastern Europe in the 1990s, the opportunity for the restoration of monarchies across the region seemed to have arrived.

In 1992, by now an elderly man, Michael was allowed to return to Romania for the first time since his abdication, and received a warm welcome from the public, with crowds said to be consisting of over a million people. Concerned by the potential destabilising effect the return of the former King could have on the fledgling new Romanian republic, the government proved hostile, with Michael prevented from returning again anytime soon. Nevertheless, five years on, Michael was permitted to return permanently, and had his former royal residences restored to him and his family. Michael now began to cooperate with the Romanian government, using his international contacts and diplomatic experience to lobby for Romania to join NATO and the European Union. Over the coming decades the Romanian royal family, and Michael in particular, found themselves in quite a unique position: whilst public scepticism of politicians and public institutions remained high, Michael and the royal family came to be exceptionally trusted and respected figures. On the occasion of his 90th birthday, Michael was permitted to make a speech to the Romanian parliament. Michael's popularity had limits though, and he did not gain enough momentum to be restored as King before his death in 2017, aged 96. Upon his return to Romania, and mindful of his advancing years, Michael had groomed his eldest child Margareta as a prospective heir, and positioned her as such in the public eye. However, it remains to be seen whether the Romanian government will pursue the subject of a restored monarchy further, or if the idea will have fundamentally been allowed to die with the former King Michael.

Zog

Despite already reaching the position of President of his country's fledgling republic, thanks in part to emphasis placed on the legacy of his illustrious ancestor, he promptly dissolved the republic he was elected to lead and instead reformed his country into a monarchy. He then orchestrated his own coronation as a royal head of state. This could outline the events in the middle of the nineteenth century surrounding Louis-Napoleon Bonaparte's emergence as Emperor Napoleon III of the French. But, in this instance, this summary is used to describe the rise of Ahmet Zogu in the 1920s, who made himself King Zog of the Albanians in 1928.

By this time, the Albanian nation had only existed as a recognised independent state for 15 years, having been established as a principality shortly before the First World War, constructed from much of the European remnants of the Ottoman Empire following the Balkan Wars. Soon after Prince William, formerly of the German state of Wied, had accepted the position of the first Prince of Albania, his new realm faced problems from inside and out. It was divided internally amongst Muslims and Christians, who had stubbornly clung on to their own traditional way of life and values during Ottoman rule, whilst this new state's integrity was soon challenged from the outside as well by neighbouring Greece and the ambitious Kingdom of Italy, which was separated from Albania by a narrow stretch of the Adriatic Sea. Moreover, the onset of the

First World War pushed Prince William to leave his young country, with the Prince of Albania never to return to his former realm. For a number of years, Albania therefore remained a principality without a prince, until giving up on the monarchy and establishing a republic in 1925.

During this time of instability in Albania, the already highborn Ahmet Zogu was able to work his way through the new country's political ranks, becoming Prime Minister in 1922. Though a quiet man, beneath the surface he proved to be remarkably steely, starkly demonstrated on one occasion in particular, when he entered the Albanian parliament as Prime Minister to make a speech, only to be shot at and wounded. This didn't stop him from delivering his speech though. When Albania became a republic in 1925, Zogu was elected as its first President, having gained renown not only for his political experience but also his noble heritage, claiming descent from the legendary medieval monarch of Albania, King Skanderbeg. Three years later, in a move reminiscent of that of Emperor Napoleon III of the French in the previous century, President Zogu took the unusual step of abolishing his own republic and making it a kingdom. Now, as King Zog, he sought to consolidate his own political power and enforce stability. In an attempt to bind the different elements of his nation together from the outset, when taking his oath as monarch King Zog pledged allegiance to his country on both the Bible and Koran.

Like many of his counterparts across Europe during the interwar period, royal and republican alike, King Zog ruled as a strongman in these unstable times. As always with authoritarian rulers, King Zog attracted strong opposition and consequently remained a prominent target for assassins, just as he had been as Prime Minister of the Albanian republic. In 1931, whilst seeing an opera in the Austrian capital, Vienna, King Zog was again targeted by an assassin, who fired a shot at the Albanian king as he was entering his car. However, for a head of state, King Zog was unusually prepared for this situation: after briefly taking cover, he then pulled out his own personal weapon, a golden gun. He then exchanged gunfire with his would-be assassin. While the reference to a golden gun conjures up connections with James Bond, King Zog's association with 007 goes intriguingly deeper: a fleeting reference to King Zog is included by author Ian Fleming in the James Bond novel, *The Man with the Golden Gun*.

Though solidarity was often demonstrated amongst monarchs, King Zog's Islamic roots and lack of family connections with European royals made him an outsider, and therefore lacked the level of support from other European monarchs some of his counterparts enjoyed. Clearly, King Zog's marriage to a Hungarian aristocrat was deemed insufficient to make him a valued member of the exclusive club of European royals. He therefore had to try harder than most as King Zog had to start from scratch when it came to forming international alliances. One country King Zog couldn't ignore was Italy, which saw Albania as part of her traditional sphere of influence, influence that was seemingly easier to exercise now that Albania was separated from the considerably larger Ottoman Empire.

King Zog was keen to preserve his country's independence, but at the same time appreciated Albania's vulnerability, hence why he cautiously encouraged close ties with his fellow strongman, Benito Mussolini, Italy's dictator. For much of the 1930s, King Zog was able to maintain friendly relations with Italy and preserve the independence of his kingdom but, as the decade drew to a close and the climate across Europe became more aggressive, King Zog grew less able to withstand increasing Italian infringement of Albanian sovereignty. Ultimately, in 1939, King Zog fled from Albania, days after the birth of his only child and heir, Prince Leka. Hot on his heels, Italian armies took over the country, and Zog was replaced as King of Albania by Italy's King Victor Emmanuel III. It is notable that there was little attempt on the part of the Albanians to try to keep Zog as King, or to resist the Italian invasion, perhaps suggesting that Zog's Kingdom of Albania had not been particularly popular.

Zog and the former Albanian royal family went into exile, but never settled in a country permanently, moving variously to Great Britain, Egypt and France. During the Second World War he awaited a restoration which never came, and all the while a communist movement gathered strength in Italian-occupied Albania. By the end of the War, the communist leader Enver Hoxha was able to emerge as Albania's new head of state, abolishing the monarchy before Zog could return. Zog died in exile in 1961. His claim was continued from overseas by his son, Crown Prince Leka, who returned to Albania in the 1990s after the fall of the communist regime in order to promote the restoration of the monarchy. Unusually, Leka's calls for a referendum on the debate were heeded, with a vote duly held in 1997. However, the referendum coincided closely with the collapse of a far-reaching pyramid finance scheme that affected a sizable proportion of the population. And so, when a clear majority voted against a restoration of the monarchy, and Leka publicly challenged the legitimacy of the result, the Albanian government had little time or patience to deal with the former royal's grievances in addition to their other pressing problems. Leka was deemed by the government to be making an already difficult time for Albania even worse and was forced into exile again; once more treated as an enemy of the Albanian state.

In the early part of the twenty-first century, relations between Albanian politicians and the former royal family improved, with Leka no longer deemed a threat and allowed to return to Albania. By now an elderly man, Leka moved further out of the spotlight as time wore on, making way for his own son, also named Leka and recognised by monarchists as Leka II, to take on a more prominent role in the monarchist cause. While the younger prince Leka achieved influence by alternative means, as a result of being hired by the government as an advisor, he inherited the claim to the former Albanian throne upon his father's death in 2011. Though generally less forceful and controversial than his father, Leka II has not only continued to advocate the restoration of the Albanian monarchy, but has even suggested that Kosovo, which has long been under Serbian influence and control, could form part of a greater prospective Kingdom of Albania, given the substantial size of Kosovo's ethnic Albanian population.

Leopold

The reign of the respected King Albert I of the Belgians, the monarch who had led his country through the hardships of the First World War, was ended abruptly and unexpectedly in 1934 when he died in a mountaineering accident. He was succeeded by his son and heir, who was crowned King Leopold III. Just over a year into King Leopold's reign, tragedy struck: whilst out driving with his wife, Queen Astrid, who was pregnant with his fourth child, King Leopold III lost control of the car, which plunged into a lake. Although the King emerged with only minor injuries, the crash killed both Queen Astrid and her unborn baby.

As with his father, King Leopold III's greatest test would be how he handled leadership of his country during a world war. Once again, Belgium was an early target for German wartime aggression, with Belgium soon overwhelmed by Nazi Germany's blitzkrieg tactics in the Second World War. However, whilst his father's reputation was bolstered in wartime, for King Leopold the subsequent war would be his undoing, and his conduct would be shrouded in controversy and mystery. When Nazi Germany annexed and occupied Belgium, King Leopold's government made their way to exile in Great Britain. King Leopold III, meanwhile, chose to remain in his country. On the face of it, it could be said that the King stayed in Belgium as a sign of solidarity with his subjects, just as King Christian X was doing in Denmark to the north. However, whilst King Christian X would receive only praise for his wartime conduct, and who remained in Denmark's collective memory as a symbol of defiance against Nazi

German occupation, rumours persisted that King Leopold III had different motives.

King Leopold III remained in German-occupied Belgium for much of the War, and on one occasion had a high-profile meeting with the Nazi German leader, Adolf Hitler. Towards the end of the War, as the Nazi German empire was falling apart, the King of the Belgians was relocated to within the borders of Nazi Germany itself, where he was ultimately located by the victorious Allied troops. Although there is agreement on King Leopold III's wartime actions, there was a lack of clarity on the motives behind these actions. Did he remain in Belgium to be with his people, or was it a sign of his willingness to collaborate with the Nazi German occupiers? Did the King meet with Hitler in order to secure better treatment of his country and his people, as he insisted, or were the ties between the Belgian monarch and German Fuhrer warmer than these apparent motives behind the meeting would suggest? And was King Leopold III relocated to Nazi Germany as a prisoner against his will, or because the Germans wanted to protect a friendly collaborator? The integrity of the King was undermined by tensions between himself and his exiled government, as well as representatives of the Allied powers. The Belgian government was critical of King Leopold's decision to remain in Belgium, and heated words were exchanged between the monarch and his government. King Leopold III was also openly hostile towards the Allies' conduct of the War, documenting his negative opinion of the Allies during the War in his *Political Testament*. In addition, whilst there had been tremendous public sympathy at the premature and tragic death of his wife, Queen Astrid, there was criticism of the timing and decision of King Leopold III to privately get remarried to a Belgian commoner, Lilian Baels, during Belgium's wartime occupation.

Though King Leopold III was found at the end of the War by the Allies, he did not immediately return to Belgium. The Allies shared the Belgian government's misgivings about the King's actions during the War, with the decision taken for King Leopold III to spend some time in exile in Switzerland whilst his brother, Prince Charles, would act as regent, and carry out royal duties on King Leopold's behalf. Over the course of the King's exile, his wartime actions and experiences would be investigated by an independent commission, to see whether he had been a willing collaborator with the Nazi German occupiers or not. A year after the War, although the commission found King Leopold III innocent of these allegations, suspicion of his conduct nevertheless remained high in Belgium; so much so that it was agreed that both King Leopold's exile and Prince Charles' regency should continue for a few more years before the King returned to his country.

In 1950, in an attempt to bring clarity to the debate, a referendum was held as to whether Leopold should be able to return and retake his position as King of the Belgians. The result was 57% in his favour, leading to Leopold's return to Belgium for the first time since the Second World War. However, the referendum, and the whole debate about King Leopold III, exposed and exacerbated clear divisions in Belgian society. Whilst it is probably unsurprising that those of Belgium's political right and left tended to be more supportive and hostile towards the King respectively, more damaging would be how the debate surrounding King Leopold highlighted the linguistic divisions in Belgium.

When Belgium became independent over a century earlier, a defining characteristic of the new country was that it was a Catholic nation that had previously been bound to the Protestant Kingdom of the Netherlands. But whilst the Belgians had been united by religion, they were divided by language and, over time, religion would play a diminishing role in Belgian society. In the north of Belgium were those identified as Flemings, who were speakers of the Flemish language that was similar to Dutch; meanwhile in the south were the Walloons, who were more linguistically akin to their French neighbours. As well as being united by religion, the Belgians were also supposed to be brought together by their monarchy. In the case of King Leopold III though there was an identifiable trend whereby he had disproportionate support from the Flemings and opposition from the Walloons. This was demonstrated upon King Leopold III's return to Belgium, when Belgium's Walloon community played an important role in strikes that were organised as a display of anger with his return. The violence and scale of the strikes escalated, and there were concerns that the full restoration of King Leopold III would divide Belgium and maybe even lead to civil war.

Talks within Belgium's ruling elite in response to these developments led to the decision of King Leopold III to abdicate in favour of his eldest son and heir who in 1951, the following year, would become King Baudouin of the Belgians. The former King Leopold would take a back seat in Belgian affairs up until his death in 1983, whilst King Baudouin became a popular monarch who restored stability to the Belgian throne. King Baudouin would largely avoid controversy except for one occasion close to the end of his reign, when his government intended to liberalise Belgian laws on abortion. This was something King

Baudouin opposed on moral grounds but, accepting that support for this move on abortion was widespread, he decided to briefly step down as King so that the new abortion laws could pass without compromising his morality. When he died in 1993 King Baudouin was succeed by his brother, King Albert II, who likewise largely avoided controversy as monarch though, at his abdication two decades later due to ill health, persistent rumours were emerging in the press that King Albert had had an illegitimate daughter, rumours the former monarch admitted were true years later after a DNA test. Following the abdication in 2013, King Albert II's son has reigned as King Philippe of the Belgians.

Peter

For several years, King Alexander I of Yugoslavia resorted to authoritarianism to hold his disunited kingdom together. Such an approach always courts controversy, particularly when the leader concerned is the embodiment of an overarching country that nationalists from competing ethnic groups wished to dissolve. Given that all these factors were coming together during Europe's inter war age of extremes, it is perhaps not altogether too surprising that, shortly after arriving in France on a state visit in 1934, King Alexander was murdered by a nationalist assassin. Officially, the heavy responsibility of holding Yugoslavia together was then inherited by his 11-year-old son, the new King Peter II; in practice, the young king's royal duties would be handled by a regent, his uncle Prince Paul, until the King was deemed to have come of age.

Yugoslavia had been established after the First World War, resulting from the union between the formerly independent kingdoms of Serbia and Montenegro, and the south Slav lands of the now defunct Austro-Hungarian Empire. The peoples of this territory largely spoke the same Slavic language, called Serbo-Croat. But despite their linguistic similarities, the people of this new country had a different past and followed different religions. This country could broadly be split in two from the outset: the northern Catholic half, which had been a Habsburg hinterland; and the south, which had been entirely self-governing since the late nineteenth century, and before that had been an

Orthodox outpost of the Ottoman Empire. The initial name of this country had been the Kingdom of Serbs, Croats and Slovenes, a name which clearly recognises the differences amongst its people. But it was also a name that did not recognise that there were further significant ethnic groups within the country's borders, which also included Macedonians and Montenegrins, to name two.

The idea was that these peoples, most of whom with a common linguistic heritage and experience of subordination in former vast empires, could now share a new country as equals. In practice, competition soon emerged between these ethnic groups for influence over the kingdom, with the Serbs often deemed to be in a stronger position from the outset, given that their House of Karadjordjevic, previously providing the kings of Serbia, would now inherit the new throne of the Kingdom of the Serbs, Croats and Slovenes. The first to do so was the former King Peter I of Serbia who, by the creation of this new kingdom, was already a quite elderly figure. Nevertheless, King Peter I was highly regarded among Serbs in particular: he had led Serbia during the crisis resulting from the assassination of Archduke Franz Ferdinand of Austria, which the overwhelming Austro-Hungarian Empire had blamed on King Peter I's country. King Peter I saw Serbia through the challenges of the First World War to ultimate victory. Moreover, despite his age, the King gained great face during the War by not only personally visiting a battlefield but also taking a rifle and firing shots at the enemy.

Although King Peter I had long been the face of first the Serbian monarchy, and then of the Kingdom of Serbs, Croats and Slovenes, for a number of years the power behind the throne had been his second son and heir, Prince Alexander, with his older brother, Prince George, having previously disgraced himself and consequently been excluded from the line of succession after he allegedly kicked a servant to death in a tantrum, and attracted widespread public scorn as a result. As has been said, whilst some saw the Kingdom of Serbs, Croats and Slovenes as the coming together of the south Slav nations in an effort to form a new country based on their commonalities; others saw this as an acquisition of new land and people, under the former Serbian royal family, by Serbia as the spoils of victory in the War. The idealistic Kingdom of Serbs, Croats and Slovenes originated as a constitutional monarchy, with the numerous different peoples of the country represented in the national parliament. However, this parliament soon became a battleground for airing jealousies and grievances between politicians reflecting competing ethnic rivalries. The parliament had almost literally become a battleground by the end of the 1920s, with threats of physical violence made between politicians. When one leading Croat politician was murdered in a parliamentary brawl in 1928 the then King Alexander I, who had finally inherited what was left of his father's power and status upon his death in 1921, felt that democracy was failing and that he was duty bound to personally make this country function, by force, if necessary. King Alexander I therefore displaced parliamentary influence with that of his own royal dictatorship. This change in power in the kingdom was marked by a new name for the country, now to be called Yugoslavia; a name that would attempt to focus on the population's similarities as south Slavs, rather than highlight the differences between them as the previous name had.

Though King Alexander I had been a unifying figure, he was also a target for determined nationalists, culminating in his assassination and bringing about the abrupt accession of King Peter II. The regency of Prince Paul during the earlier years of King Peter II's reign struggled to keep Yugoslavia together, with the Croats making the most progress in splitting the country and seemed to be on the cusp of gaining concessions of national autonomy by the late 1930s. The nationalist divisions of Yugoslavia would go from bad to worse with the onset of the Second World War. As the War spread across the continent and grew harder to ignore, Yugoslavia became even more divided as to how to respond, even exposing divisions within the royal family. Those resolutely opposed to reaching any form of understanding with the Axis Powers, whose armies were moving closer to Yugoslavia's borders, were increasingly rallying around the young King Peter II; Prince Paul meanwhile, in a move that was said to be more out of pragmatism than principle, was concluding an understanding with Nazi Germany and Fascist Italy. When these efforts resulted in a pact between these countries, a coup deposed Prince Paul and King Peter II was hastily declared of age to rule Yugoslavia by himself, despite being just 17 years old. However principled the uprising against the pact with the Axis Powers may have been, this coup had the consequence of prompting an invasion of Yugoslavia by the Axis Powers, who dismembered the country to suit their own ends. Exploiting Yugoslavia's divisions, the Axis occupiers wooed potential supporters by playing to nationalists' demands, with Italy sponsoring a number of sympathetic monarchies to replace the former Kingdom of Yugoslavia. These included a Croatian kingdom, to be ruled by King Victor Emmanuel III of Italy's nephew, Aimone, Duke of Spoleto; as well as a restored Kingdom of Montenegro, with the intention of bringing in the heir to the former Montenegrin throne, Prince Michael, who also happened to be the Queen of Italy's nephew, as king.

Meanwhile King Peter II went to Great Britain in exile, where he developed warm relations with the leaders of the Allies. Although Yugoslavia was a divided country, with these divisions exploited by the Axis Powers, there were still those who supported the idea of a united Yugoslavia, and would fight to restore the country's integrity and independence. These included the Chetniks, who were monarchists led by Dragoljub Mihailovic, that wanted to bring back King Peter II and his Kingdom of Yugoslavia; they also included the Partisans, who hoped to make Yugoslavia into a communist state, led by Josip Broz Tito. As supporters of a previously established system, and backed by an exiled government and king that had the ear of the Allies, Mihailovic's Chetniks had the upper hand as they began the fight for Yugoslavia's post war future, while King Peter's good relations with the Allies secured material support for the Chetniks' resistance movement. In fact, so warm were the ties cultivated by King Peter II that, as a sign of goodwill, when Queen Alexandra, wife of King Peter II and daughter of King Alexander I of Greece, gave birth to their only child and heir, Crown Prince Alexander, in a London hotel room, British Prime Minister Winston Churchill temporarily ceded the space that the hotel room occupied to Yugoslavia so that it could be said that the heir was born on Yugoslavian territory. The Crown Prince's godparents included Great Britain's King George VI, as well as his daughter, the future Queen Elizabeth II.

As the War continued however, there would be a growing disparity between the close ties of the Yugoslavian royal family with the Allies over in Great Britain, and the efforts for restored Yugoslav independence back at home. Increasingly, the Chetniks were treating Tito's Partisans as the greater enemy, to the point where there were growing indications of Chetnik collaboration with the Axis Powers at the Partisans' expense. The Chetniks also seemed to be ineffective in uniting the ethnic groups of Yugoslavia, more often coming across as Serbian nationalists instead. Moreover, the Chetniks appeared in a poor light when contrasted with Tito's Partisans, who were relentlessly focused on and opposed to Axis forces, and included a range of Yugoslavs (so not just relying on Serbs) among their backers. The Allies, despite their personal relationship with King Peter II, could not ignore these developments, and in the latter years of the War felt compelled to shift their support from the Chetniks to the Partisans. Then by the end of the War, the Allies came out as supporting Josip Broz Tito to become Yugoslavia's post-war leader, who brought the country together again as a communist state that abolished the monarchy. This left King Peter II exiled overseas, where he would remain for the rest of his life, bewildered by these developments in his homeland that were out of his hands, until his death in 1970.

The cause of a restored monarchy has since been enthusiastically promoted by his son, Crown Prince Alexander. Monarchism appeared to be a hopeless cause while Tito remained in power, who proved to be an effective unifying figure for Yugoslavia. But in the decade that followed Tito's death in 1980 Yugoslavia began to show signs of fragmentation and, with the fall of communism around her elsewhere in Eastern Europe, nationalism emerged in communism's stead, rearing its ugly head in Yugoslavian politics again at the turn of the 1990s. Most of the different ethnic groups of Yugoslavia would soon set up new republics of their own, breaking away from the divisive rule of Slobodan Milosevic. By the arrival of the twenty-first century the process seemed to be nearing its end, with the resignation of Milosevic a significant milestone in the year 2000.

All the while, Crown Prince Alexander had been reviewing events from the side-lines and, perhaps controversially as a prospective constitutional monarch, would share opinions on contemporary Yugoslavia, for example criticising Milosevic. In 2001 Crown Prince Alexander relocated himself and his family to Yugoslavia and, with the final dissolution of the union between Serbia and Montenegro in 2006, the Crown Prince asserted himself as Serbia's prospective head of state and as a peaceful champion of Serbian national identity. Crown Prince Alexander and his family have taken an active role in Serbian society, supporting various charitable and national causes, hoping to keep themselves in the public eye and endear themselves to Serbians in order to encourage a restoration of the monarchy in Serbia, with the Crown Prince hoping to be crowned King Alexander II. Opinion polls over the past decade have shown that there is at least some consistent support for such a restoration, but it is unclear whether Crown Prince Alexander's efforts will bear fruit whilst he is alive (he is now in his 70s), or if instead, reminiscent of the late former King Michael of Romania, he will never quite achieve his lifelong ambition.

Rainier

Fortunately, by the death of Prince Louis II of Monaco in 1949, his country had long been prepared to avert the succession crisis that could have otherwise occurred. As Prince Louis II had approached middle age without legitimate offspring, there was concern over who would succeed him. Whilst it was always expected that his successor would have the blood of the Grimaldi dynasty in their veins, they would also have to be acceptable to not only the Monegasque people but additionally the government of Monaco's overwhelming neighbour, France. A succession crisis was averted when Charlotte, Prince Louis II's illegitimate daughter, was legitimised by the Prince adopting her, which led to Charlotte's formal recognition as a princess and as his heir. When her own son, Prince Rainier, reached his 21st birthday in 1944, Princess Charlotte renounced her position in the Monegasque line of succession, making Prince Rainier heir to the throne that he would inherit five years later.

During his lengthy reign, Prince Rainier III made significant changes to his country. He acted to curtail his own political powers, which were extensive, in favour of an elected National Council. But whilst Prince Rainier reduced his formal powers by his own accord, he would continue to still exercise considerable influence. As one of Europe's smallest independent countries, Monaco needed to be imaginative to sustain economic activity there. Already the

Monaco Grand Prix attracted global interest, and the Principality's well-established casino had become world famous. But Prince Rainier was keen to diversify his country's economy beyond its reliance on gambling, a source of income which was hit hard by the world wars and increasingly undermined by the growth of other gambling centres around the world. Prince Rainier III therefore tried to bring in tourists beyond noble Europeans by promoting Monaco's reputation as a tax haven to attract wealthy long-term residents. He was also able to exercise more control over Monaco's economic future when he eventually managed to stifle the growing influence of the rich shipping magnate, Aristotle Onassis, over the Societe des Bains de Mer. The Societe des Bains de Mer, or SBM, is the company that has historically controlled (and continues to control) a number of Monaco's leading tourist attractions, including hotels such as the Hotel de Paris, and casinos like the Monte Carlo Casino, arguably Monaco's most famous landmark.

One of Prince Rainier III's life decisions also helped provide an enduring link for Monaco with celebrity glamour, adding to the Principality's existing royal spectacle. The once very separate spheres of royalty and celebrity have begun to blur in modern times; something perhaps to be expected, given how the role of monarchy has changed. Whereas they once exercised significant, often authoritarian, power over their countries, royals have for the most part seen their influence dwindle in the modern era, with their former decision-making duties since inherited by democratically elected politicians. A number of monarchies also became republics, transforming the livelihoods of even more royals. Given this loss of political power, royals found their positions becoming more symbolic instead and focused on image. Later in the twentieth century, this trend would coincide with the explosion in the pervasiveness of the media in people's everyday lives, which highly prized gossip about the rich and famous, while fashion magazines would showcase royalty side by side with television personalities and celebrities. Though most recently this blurring of the worlds of royalty and celebrity was illustrated by the wedding of Prince Harry, a high-profile member of the British royal family, to American actress, Meghan Markle, in 2018, it is Prince Rainier III of Monaco who provided one of the earlier and most grand examples of this. In 1956, Prince Rainier III married Grace Kelly, a young American actress who gained global fame as a Hollywood star, appearing in a number of popular and successful films in the early 1950s. Their marriage would instigate and sustain even more worldwide interest in Prince Rainier's tiny principality. Over the decades ahead, Monaco's royal couple exploited the global attention they attracted to promote the interests of their country and other causes; but this was sadly cut short by the premature death of Princess Grace in 1982, following complications after a car crash.

Prince Rainier III would go on to be amongst the longest reigning monarchs in modern times but, unlike his predecessor, was not in danger of provoking a succession crisis, having fathered three children with Princess Grace, including his son and heir, Prince Albert. When Prince Rainier's health began to deteriorate at the beginning of the twenty-first century, Prince Albert was able to assume his duties on his father's behalf when required, and inherited the throne upon Prince Rainier III's death in 2005, after a reign of over 50 years. At his death Prince Rainier could be satisfied with his legacy, being that, in the face of great international competition, Monaco would nevertheless sustain its global reputation as a hub for the rich and famous, continuing to attract many wealthy investors, residents and tourists.

Recalling past concerns with the Monegasque monarchy, the media began to speculate about another succession crisis in the event that the new Prince Albert II of Monaco, a renowned bachelor, did not soon find a wife, given that he was now approaching middle age, echoing the case of his great-grandfather, Prince Louis II. The intense media attention relented though after Prince Albert II managed to find a bride, one who was also already familiar with being in the public gaze. Prince Albert II married South African athlete, Charlene Wittstock, in 2011, and a few years later she gave birth to twins, Prince Jacques and Princess Gabriella. Monaco's laws of succession make Prince Jacques first in line to the throne, followed by his twin sister.

Juan Carlos

The conclusion of the First World War appeared to mark a clear beginning for the end of monarchy as an institution in favour of republics, coinciding with the dissolution of several of Europe's most prominent empires, including Russia, Germany and Austria-Hungary, then the Ottoman Empire soon afterwards. Smaller republics tended to take their place. The Second World War then seemed to confirm this apparently inevitable decline, thanks in part to the fall of fascism, affecting those monarchies tainted by this ideology, and the rise of communism, as the Soviet Union's government imposed communist dictatorships on the countries it was located closely to, or home-grown communists were simply inspired by the Soviet example and used the War as an opportunity to gain control whilst their monarchs were exiled overseas. The establishment of a republic in Greece in 1974, with King Constantine II of Greece having done irreparable damage to the reputation of himself and the monarchy by supporting a military coup in 1967, marked another significant milestone, as Greece had been the last monarchy in Eastern Europe, while the loss of the Greek monarchy also brought the total of hereditary monarchies in Europe down to single figures. However, in a swift rebuff to this trend, in 1975, just a year after Greece voted to replace the monarchy with a republic, Juan Carlos was crowned the first King of Spain in decades.

Spain was historically a well-established kingdom, and indeed had been one of the most powerful countries in the world during the early modern era, overseeing an empire that covered much of South America and penetrated deeply into North America as well. Though the Spanish Empire was greatly diminished, and the monarchy shaken, during the course of the nineteenth century, in the early part of the twentieth century the Kingdom of Spain seemed to be in a stronger position than most in some respects: while most European countries were exhausted by the First World War, Spain had taken the quite exceptional step of remaining neutral during this conflict. Meanwhile in contrast to Greece at this time, where the monarchy was remarkably unstable and the Greek crown was frequently passed from one king to another, Spain had consistently remained under Alfonso XIII. King of Spain literally from his birth in 1886, as his father and predecessor King Alfonso XII died several months before he was born, Alfonso XIII would reign until 1931.

Unlike most royal reigns though, it was not death that stopped King Alfonso XIII's rule. Despite Spain being in a relatively strong position following the First World War, she was not immune to the continent-wide challenges of the interwar period, and in 1923 King Alfonso XIII was quick to support the military coup and dictatorship of General Miguel Primo de Rivera. Far from being anxious about supporting such a move, King Alfonso XIII was proud of Primo de Rivera's regime, boastfully describing the dictator as "my Mussolini", alluding to the relationship between his Italian counterpart, King Victor Emmanuel III, and Benito Mussolini. As this would suggest, King Alfonso XIII aligned himself closely with Primo de Rivera and, when Spanish resentment towards the dictatorship grew overwhelming, particularly as their country was impacted by the 1929 Wall Street Crash, Primo de Rivera stepped down as dictator a year later. Hostility towards Primo de Rivera and his regime was also directed at the King, as was evident in the 1931 elections, which saw republican political parties win by a landslide. In response, King Alfonso XIII fled and Spain became a republic. However, whilst the Spanish at the time seemed united in wanting to force King Alfonso XIII from the throne, there were divisions over who and what should succeed him, culminating in the Spanish Civil War in 1936. This pitted left wing republicans and socialists against right wing ultra-conservatives and fascists. Notably, neither side fought for a restoration of the monarchy. The scale of the conflict escalated in significance as international powers intervened, with the Soviet Union backing the left, while the right, led by General Francisco Franco, was supported by Fascist Italy and Nazi Germany.

The right ultimately triumphed but curiously, while it could have been anticipated that Franco would have brought Spain into the Second World War on the side of the Axis Powers that had backed him during the Civil War, he instead kept his country formally neutral, as it had been in the previous war. This neutrality, and the perception of Franco's right-wing dictatorship by the United States and others as a lesser evil than a communist state during the subsequent Cold War, helped Franco's regime long outlast those of his fascist counterparts, Mussolini and Adolf Hitler. From the 1960s into the 1970s, as he entered old age General Franco began planning for his succession. Whilst he was a traditionalist, and sympathiser with the institution of monarchy, Franco was also determined that the regime he had established should fundamentally be preserved after his death. With the former King Alfonso XIII having died in exile in 1941, his son, Prince Juan, had since asserted himself as heir to the Spanish throne. However, Franco perceived Prince Juan as a liberal who would promptly undermine his ambitions for the continuation of his regime after his death, so Franco looked elsewhere for a new Spanish monarch to succeed him. However, Franco was repeatedly steered towards Prince Juan Carlos, Prince Juan's son. Franco therefore took Prince Juan Carlos under his wing, grooming him to uphold his right-wing dictatorship, which the Prince seemed very willing and able to do.

When the inevitable happened in 1975 and General Franco passed away, the new King Juan Carlos of Spain was widely expected to preserve the status quo of Franco's right-wing regime. Instead, King Juan Carlos did the opposite, swiftly dismantling the institutions of dictatorship and restoring free elections, revoking the restrictions Franco's regime had placed on political parties, including those on the political left. Whilst many Spaniards, and international observers, were pleasantly surprised by these developments, others, particularly left wingers, were more wary and sceptical as to the depth of King Juan Carlos' democratic convictions. In 1981, this was put to the test. Influential supporters of Franco's regime still remained, notably in the military, and were appalled with the democratic direction King Juan Carlos had taken Spain in, so an uprising was arranged to restore a government more like that of General Franco's, and providing King Juan Carlos with an opportunity to change course. The initial steps for this coup were therefore taken, and King Juan Carlos needed to react. Looking to the precedents set by several of his royal counterparts in recent history, including his grandfather King Alfonso XIII in the 1920s, and his brother-in-law, King Constantine II of Greece, just over a decade before, this seemed to be King Juan Carlos' chance to support yet another European military dictatorship. The King's reaction was to make contact with the leading members of the military, but to encourage them to support the restored democracy in Spain. The King then made a public broadcast, pledging his support for democracy, opposition to the coup, and his hope that the public would back him. The coup duly fell, and praise was heaped upon King Juan Carlos: a modern monarch who appeared to have learnt the lessons of history. Across the political spectrum, King Juan Carlos' handling of the coup and restoration of democracy drew respect.

In fact, in the decades ahead, King Juan Carlos of Spain would remain a highly regarded figure not only in Spain but internationally, particularly in the Spanish-speaking world. However, while King Juan Carlos' actions would not be forgotten, public gratitude would only go so far. In the early twenty-first century, age had dampened the energy of King Juan Carlos, while Spain was hit particularly hard by the Great Recession, souring the mood of many Spaniards. There was therefore little sympathy for the King when, in 2012, he sustained an injury whilst elephant hunting in Botswana, an activity that seemed drastically out of touch with the public. Not only was it seen as an unnecessary extravagance at a time of financial hardship at home, it was also deemed distasteful for King Juan Carlos to be hunting elephants, particularly as president of the World Wildlife Fund in Spain. As a result of this incident, King Juan Carlos was obliged to make a public apology. Over the next couple of years, in declining health and with dented prestige, while at the same time seeing the smooth transitions from one generation of monarchy to the next in the Netherlands and Belgium, it was decided that it would be best for King Juan Carlos to follow suit and abdicate in favour of his son, who became King Felipe VI of Spain in 2014. Although the transition wasn't quite as trouble-free as the Spanish royals had hoped, with public demonstrations for a republic (or at least a referendum on the matter) in the wake of the announcement of King Juan Carlos' abdication, King Felipe VI was personally a popular figure, and soon gained acceptance as Spain's monarch. Though a constitutional monarch, expected to take a backseat in politics, King Felipe VI would have to respond carefully to those challenges Spain shared with other European countries, namely the Great Recession and migrant crisis, as well as to those more specific to his country, with the movement for Catalan independence a particular concern.

Mindful of his responsibility to be objective in politics, King Felipe VI nevertheless deemed it appropriate to take sides in the Catalan separatist dilemma, as an unofficial referendum on independence was held in 2017 and violent clashes occurred between demonstrators favouring the independence of Catalonia and the police. In a broadcast, King Felipe VI criticised the demonstrators and called for Spanish unity. It is not without precedent for constitutional monarchs to appear to take sides in political debates that concern the integrity of their country though. In 2014, when the famously impartial Queen Elizabeth II of Great Britain was informed by the Prime Minister, David Cameron, that Scotland had voted in the referendum to remain within the United Kingdom, even she is said to have 'purred' with happiness at the result.

Gallery

NAPOLEON I
Emperor of the French

CARL XIV
King of Sweden

LOUIS PHILIPPE
King of the French

OTTO
King of Greece

VICTORIA
Queen of Great Britain

FRANZ JOSEPH
Emperor of Austria and Ireland

NAPOLEON III
Emperor of the French

ALEXANDER II
Tsar of Russia

HENRI
Count of Chambord

NIKOLA I
Prince of Montenegro

FRIEDRICH III
Emperor of Germany

WILHELMINA
Queen of the Netherlands

NICHOLAS II VICTOR EMMANUEL III
Tsar of Russia King of Italy

King Victor Emmanuel III of Italy GEORGE V
With King Albert I of the Belgians King of Great
This picture highlights Britain and Ireland
The Italian monarch's short stature

King George V
of Great Britain and
Ireland with Tsar Nicholas II of Russia.
Note their remarkable physical similarity

CHRISTIAN X
King of Denmark

KARL
Emperor of Austria-Hungary

'MINDAUGAS II'
Duke Wilhelm of Urach

'VASYL'
Archduke Wilhelm

OTTO
von Habsburg of Austria

MICHAEL
King of Romania

ZOG
King of the Albanians

LEOPOLD III
King of the Belgians

PETER II
King of Yugoslavia

RAINIER III
Prince of Monaco

JUAN CARLOS
King of Spain

Appendix I
Europe's Royal Houses

Given that there are many royal houses and countries in Europe, what follows is only a selection based on those that have formed the focus of this book. For each dynasty there will be a brief description of its roots and the countries it has led. There will then be an outline of the monarchs from that royal house that have either reigned or at least claimed a throne in a country covered by this book, whilst those royals with their own dedicated chapter appear in bold. Royal titles will be included when they have actually been head of state, while royal titles will accordingly be missed when the throne has been lost and an individual is only a claimant. The years stated beside each royal will cover the time they held a throne, or a claim to a throne, for. Short-lived monarchies that received little formal recognition, such as the wartime Kingdom of Lithuania, are not included. Similarly, whilst monarchs and pretenders can be recognised in their respective positions for many years, and maybe several decades; on the other hand, this status may also be only held briefly. Therefore, whenever a reign or claim lasts for less than a month, it will not be included. Please also note that, while some monarchies might be newly established, their monarchs may have chosen to be numbered according to the states that preceded the new monarchy. For example, the Kings of Italy also take into account the numbering applicable to the preceding Kings of Piedmont-Sardinia.

Although this book provides a general overview, and covers most major European monarchies in the modern era, it is worth bearing in mind that there are some notable omissions. For example, Portugal was a well-established kingdom up until the revolution that established the republic there in 1910, while the Ottoman Empire, led by the House of Osman, lasted until 1922, when it was reformed into the Republic of Turkey. Meanwhile, although most of the European monarchies still in existence today have been covered in some detail, you will note others have only been briefly mentioned, or not mentioned at all. Aside from what could be considered as two non-hereditary monarchies, including the Vatican City, where the Pope is chosen by senior members of the Catholic Church, and Andorra, which has two co-princes, which are the French head of state and the Bishop of Urgell from Spain, Europe's other monarchies, where the position of head of state is hereditary, still in existence today include:

Kingdom of Belgium
Kingdom of Denmark
United Kingdom of Great Britain and Northern Ireland
Principality of Liechtenstein
Grand Duchy of Luxembourg
Principality of Monaco
Kingdom of the Netherlands
Kingdom of Norway
Kingdom of Spain
Kingdom of Sweden

House of Bernadotte

Established when Jean Bernadotte, who served as one of the elite Marshals of Napoleon's First French Empire, was invited by the government of Sweden to become their king, in anticipation of the extinction of Sweden's reigning House of Holstein-Gottorp. Whilst Bernadotte, who became King Karl XIV of Sweden, was also initially King of Norway as well, Norway voted for independence in 1905 and established a monarchy of its own, leaving Sweden as the last realm of the House of Bernadotte. Nevertheless, ever since it was established, the Bernadotte dynasty has retained the Swedish throne.

HOUSE OF HOLSTEIN-GOTTORP

King Karl XIV of Sweden-Norway	1818–1844
King Oscar I	1844–1859
King Karl XV	1859–1872
King Oscar II	1872–1905

King Oscar II of Sweden	1905–1907
King Gustav V	1907–1950
King Gustav VI	1950–1973
King Karl XVI	1973–

House Of Bonaparte

The reach of the House of Bonaparte has been widespread in Europe, but also short-lived. Stemming from the establishment of the First French Empire by Napoleon Bonaparte, who crowned himself Emperor of the French, his empire's borders continued to stretch deeper into Europe as the earlier years of his reign progressed, while the Bonapartes' sphere of influence spread even further thanks in part to the satellite states they established, with members of the Bonaparte dynasty imposed on these states. Though this period in the early nineteenth century would mark the peak of the House of Bonaparte's influence, it was not quite the end. In the middle of the nineteenth century, the first Emperor Napoleon's nephew became Emperor Napoleon III of the French. Whilst his Second French Empire didn't have the same far-reaching impact of the First, it nevertheless managed to rule France for longer, and instead had a more subtle influence on the rest of Europe, notably by way of Emperor Napoleon III's role in the unification of what would become the Kingdom of Italy.

FIRST FRENCH REPUBLIC

Emperor Napoleon I of the French   1804–1814

HOUSE OF BOURBON

Emperor Napoleon I   –1815

HOUSES OF BOURBON AND ORLEANS
AND SECONDFRENCH REPUBLIC

Napoleon I   1815–1821
Napoleon II   1821–1832
Joseph I   (King Jose I of Spain)   1832–1844
Louis I (King Louis I of the Netherlands)   1844–1846
Napoleon III   1846–1852
Emperor Napoleon III   1852–1870

THIRD FRENCH REPUBLIC

Napoleon III   1870–1873
Napoleon IV   1873–1879
Napoleon V   1879–1891
Napoleon VI   1891–1926
Napoleon VII   1926–1997
Napoleon VIII   1997–

KINGDOM OF PIEDMONT-SARDINIA and other Italian states

King Napoleon I of Italy   1805–1814

KINGDOM OF PIEDMONT-SARDINIA and other Italian states

BATAVIAN REPUBLIC

King Louis I of Holland   1806–1810

FIRST FRENCH EMPIRE

HOUSE OF BOURBON

King Jose I of Spain   1808–1813

HOUSE OF BOURBON

House of Bourbon

Of French origin, the Bourbon dynasty reigned in France for centuries, and over time also came to rule Spain, overseeing both countries from the early modern period into the modern era. Bourbons would also reign in some of the smaller monarchies that preceded the unification of Italy, including the Kingdom of Two Sicilies in the south of the peninsula and the Duchy of Parma in the north. Whilst these two Italian monarchies were dissolved due to the unification of Italy under the House of Savoy, the Parma branch has managed to retain another throne to the present day thanks to the marriage of Grand Duchess Charlotte of Luxembourg to Felix of Parma, meaning that the Bourbons have reigned in the Grand Duchy of Luxembourg ever since. During the nineteenth century, the Bourbons were in the thick of the frequent regime changes in France, with King Charles X the last Bourbon King of France, while his grandson, Henri of Chambord, was widely considered the last of the French Bourbons, who missed the opportunity to be restored as King of France largely due to a clash of principles between himself and the French government in the latter part of the nineteenth century, as symbolised by their debate over the French flag. Though Bourbons would continue to claim the French throne after Henri's death, this branch is in reality more Spanish than French. Meanwhile, though the Bourbons lost the Spanish throne with the fall of King Alfonso XIII at the onset of the

1930s, they were returned with the restoration of the monarchy under King Juan Carlos in 1975.

King Louis XVI of France   1774–1791
King Louis XVI of the French   1791–1792

FIRST FRENCH REPUBLIC AND HOUSE OF BONAPARTE

Louis XVII of France   1793–1795
Louis XVIII   1795–1814
King Louis XVIII   1814–1815

HOUSE OF BONAPARTE

King Louis XVIII   1815–1824
King Charles X   1824–1830

HOUSE OF ORLEANS

Charles X   1830–1836
Louis XIX   1836–1844
Henri V   1844–1883
(Extinct)

King Carlos IV of Spain   1788–1808
King Fernando VII   1808

HOUSE OF BONAPARTE

King Fernando VII   1813–1833
Queen Isabella II   1833–1868

PROVISIONAL GOVERNMENT, HOUSE OF SAVOY
AND FIRST SPANISH REPUBLIC

King Alfonso XII   1874–1885
King Alfonso XIII   1886–1931

SECOND SPANISH REPUBLIC AND FRANCOIST
SPAIN

King Juan Carlos I   1975–2014
King Felipe VI   2014–

House of Glucksburg

The House of Glucksburg inherited the Danish throne upon the extinction of the reigning House of Oldenburg in 1863. Though Prince Christian of the House of Glucksburg was already related to the ailing King Frederick VII of Denmark when he was appointed heir to the Danish throne, his position was boosted by his choice of Princess Louise of Hesse-Kassel as his wife, given that she was even more closely connected to the Danish royals than Prince Christian as the niece of King Christian VIII of Denmark. The new King Christian IX of Denmark promptly extended the reach of the House of Glucksburg, once only a junior dynasty in Denmark, thanks not only to his descendants' retention of the Danish throne, but also his dynasty's selection to provide monarchs for the Kingdom of Greece and Kingdom of Norway, starting with one of his sons becoming King George I of Greece, then one of his grandsons becoming King Haakon VII of Norway. Furthermore, King Christian IX's other offspring also married into other European royal households, earning him the nickname the 'Father-in-law of Europe'. Whilst the Glucksburgs' reign in Greece would end in 1974, with the establishment of the country's present-day republic, the tradition of members of the dynasty marrying into other royal families has led to Greek royals holding prominent positions elsewhere in Europe, with Princess Sofia of Greece marrying King Juan Carlos and becoming Queen of Spain, whilst Prince Philip of Greece married Queen Elizabeth II of Great Britain and became

Duke of Edinburgh. Meanwhile, the House of Glucksburg continues to hold the thrones of Denmark and Norway.

HOUSE OF OLDENBURG

King Christian IX of Denmark   1863–1906
King Frederick VIII   1906–1912
King Christian X   1912–1918
King Christian X of Denmark and Iceland 1918–1944
King Christian X of Denmark   1944–1947
King Frederick IX   1947–1972
Queen Margrethe II   1972–

HOUSE OF WITTELSBACH

King George I of the Hellenes   1863–1913
King Constantine I   1913–1917
King Alexander I   1917–1920
King Constantine I   1920–1922
King George II   1922–1924

SECOND HELLENIC REPUBLIC

King George II	1935–1947
King Paul I	1947–1964
King Constantine II	1964–1973
Constantine II	1973–

House of Grimaldi

Though for many centuries associated with Monaco, this dynasty was of Italian origin, with the Genoese Grimaldi family taking control of Monaco in the thirteenth century, and holding the title of Prince of Monaco from the seventeenth century. Though the House of Grimaldi has retained the throne of Monaco since, it has come close to losing it at times, notably with the succession crisis in the earlier part of the twentieth century, when there was a chance that a member of the German House of Urach could have inherited the Monegasque crown. However, a series of written agreements during the twentieth century provided greater clarity for the Monegasque monarchy, including on the line of succession, the role of neighbouring France, and on the subject of Monaco's continued independence.

Prince Honore III of Monaco   1733–1793

FIRST FRENCH REPUBLIC AND FIRST FRENCH EMPIRE

Prince Honore IV   1814–1819
Prince Honore V   1819–1841
Prince Florestan I   1841–1856
Prince Charles III   1856–1889
Prince Albert I   1889–1922
Prince Louis II   1922–1949
Prince Rainier III   1949–2005
Prince Albert II   2005–

House of Habsburg

A formidable royal house whose heyday was in early modern times, when the Habsburgs not only commanded the extensive Holy Roman Empire across Central Europe, but would at times also hold the Spanish throne, which meant that the Habsburgs additionally oversaw Spain's vast overseas empire that covered much of South America. Though the Spanish Habsburgs would die out, leaving the Spanish throne to the Bourbons, first the House of Habsburg, then via the House of Habsburg-Lorraine, would endure for longer in the country with which it would become synonymous: Austria. Though the Holy Roman Empire, then Austrian Empire, would face great challenges in the nineteenth century, it managed to not only survive but continued to play a key role in European affairs during this period. Whilst the partnership of Emperor Francis and his chancellor, Klemens von Metternich, would bolster Habsburg power in the early nineteenth century, Europe's revolutionary tide battered the Habsburgs more than most. Bringing down Metternich and the enfeebled Emperor Ferdinand, the 1848 revolutions made way for Emperor Franz Joseph, who would see the Habsburg Empire into the twentieth century. The Habsburgs would attempt to extend their influence further, but with little success, with a brief foray back into the Americas, with Maximilian, Emperor Franz Joseph's younger brother, becoming Emperor of Mexico in the 1860s while, during the First World War, they also hoped to make much of Eastern Europe a Habsburg sphere of influence. This would have been achieved by their plans to install Austrian archdukes as monarchs in prospective Kingdoms of Poland and Ukraine, to stand shoulder to shoulder with the young reformist Emperor Karl of Austria-Hungary. However, wartime defeat spelt the end for Habsburg rule, despite fleeting opportunities for a restoration during the interwar period.

Emperor Joseph II of the Holy Roman Empire	1764–1790
Emperor Leopold II	1790–1792
Emperor Francis II	1792–1806
Emperor Francis I of Austria	1804–1835
Emperor Ferdinand I	1835–1848
Emperor Franz Joseph I	1848–1867
Emperor Franz Joseph I of Austria-Hungary	1867–1916
Emperor Karl I	1916–1918

REPUBLIC OF AUSTRIA AND other Central European states

Karl I	1918–1922
Otto I	1922–2007
Karl II	2007–

House of Hanover

Though the royals of the German state of Hanover would rise in prominence in their homeland, becoming Kings of Hanover in the nineteenth century, the Hanoverian dynasty reached global exposure once they inherited the British throne towards the end of the early modern period, and in turn became the faces of the worldwide British Empire. For a time, the head of the House of Hanover would be head of state of both Hanover and Great Britain, but the differing laws of succession in these countries meant that, when King William died in 1837, his brother Ernest Augustus became King of Hanover, while his niece became Queen Victoria of Great Britain. Though Queen Victoria reigned during the House of Hanover's peak, adding the status of Empress of India to the collection of royal titles the royal house held, her death also marked its demise as her son, King Edward VII, took the name of her husband's dynasty, the House of Saxe-Coburg-Gotha. Meanwhile, the royal state from which they took their name had by this time long been dissolved, as the Kingdom of Hannover was absorbed into the Kingdom of Prussia in 1866 during the Wars of German Unification.

King George III of Great Britain	1760–1800
King George III of Great Britain and Ireland	1801–1820
King George IV	1820–1830
King William IV	1830–1837
Queen Victoria	1837–1901

HOUSE OF SAXE-COBURG-GOTHA

House of Hohenzollern

Over the centuries, the House of Hohenzollern emerged as the ruling dynasty of the Kingdom of Prussia, which at the onset of the nineteenth century increasingly rivalled the traditional dominance of the Habsburg Empire in Central Europe. The middle of the century saw the competition between the realms of the Hohenzollerns and the Habsburgs reach a crescendo in the Austro-Prussian War. Prussia's victory set it firmly on the road to establishing a German Empire, to be dominated by the Hohenzollern-led Prussia, as steered by Chancellor Otto von Bismarck, while the defeated Habsburg, Emperor Franz Joseph, struggled to hold his empire together. With the rise of Prussia came the accompanying rise of the Hohenzollerns, with King Wilhelm I of Prussia also becoming Emperor Wilhelm I of Germany. It was during the German Wars of Unification that another member of the Hohenzollern dynasty, Prince Karl, was invited to reign over the emerging Balkan state of Romania. He accepted the offer and would become King Carol I of Romania. Though associated with conservatism and hostility to liberalism, thanks to the reputations of the German emperors Wilhelm I and Wilhelm II, there was a potential window of change that came to a swift close thanks to the premature death of Emperor Friedrich III, after a reign lasting a matter of months. Despite the family bond between them, national interests appeared to take priority as the Hohenzollern monarchs of Germany and Romania became enemies during the First World War. Though the Kingdom of

Romania was the more junior state in the European power rankings, their branch of the House of Hohenzollern emerged stronger as they were part of the victorious alliance of Entente Powers, and saw the significant expansion of their territory at the expense of the defeated Habsburg Empire. Meanwhile, Germany's Hohenzollerns were dethroned at the War's end, along with the country's other more junior royals, sending the former Emperor Wilhelm II of Germany to exile in the Kingdom of the Netherlands for the rest of his life.

KINGDOM OF PRUSSIA and other German states

Emperor Wilhelm I of Germany	1871–1888
Emperor Friedrich III	1888
Emperor Wilhelm II	1888–1918

REPUBLIC OF GERMANY (Weimar Republic)

Wilhelm II	1918–1941
Wilhelm III	1941–1951
Ludwig Ferdinand	1951–1994
Georg Friedrich	1994–

OTTOMAN EMPIRE

Prince Carol I of Romania	1877–1881
King Carol I of Romania	1881–1914

King Ferdinand	1914–1927
King Michael	1927–1930
King Carol II	1930–1940
King Michael	1940–1947

SOCIALIST REPUBLIC OF ROMANIA

Michael	1947–2017
Margareta	2017–

House of Karadjordjevic

From Serbia's fight for independence from the Ottoman Empire emerged the families of Karadjordjevic and Obrenovic as national heroes. As Serbia's degree of self-government expanded in the nineteenth century, these two families became rival royal houses to lead this new state. Whilst the House of Obrenovic oversaw Serbia's international recognition as an independent country, and received the later boost from a principality to a kingdom, their controversial King Alexander was murdered along with his queen in murky circumstances in 1903, allowing Peter, head of the House of Karadjordjevic, to be crowned King of Serbia. Despite having spent most of his life waiting in the wings, King Peter ascended the throne at an important time, just over a decade before the First World War: a conflict that would make or break his country. Following the War, King Peter was not only King of the Serbs, but also of the Croats and Slovenes, in an expanded realm that would be renamed the Kingdom of Yugoslavia under his son and successor, King Alexander I. Whilst the House of Karadjordjevic did well out of the First World War, the same could certainly not be said of the Second, as the young King Peter II was exiled, never to return, as his country was dismembered by the Axis Powers. Despite initial assurances of restoration from the Allied Powers, this stance was reversed as the War continued; and when Yugoslavia was brought together again at the end of the War, it was as a communist state. Today, King Peter II's son and heir, Alexander, enthusiastically campaigns for the restoration of the monarchy in the present-day Republic of Serbia.

HOUSE OF OBRENOVIC	

King Peter I of Serbia	1903–1918
King Peter I of Serbs, Croats and Slovenes	1918–1921
King Alexander I	1921–1929
King Alexander I of Yugoslavia	1929–1934
King Peter II	1934–1945

SOCIALIST FEDERAL REPUBLIC OF YUGOSLAVIA	

Peter II	1945–1970
Alexander II	1970–2006
Alexander II of Serbia	2006–

House of Orange

The House of Orange has played a prominent role in the Netherlands since early modern times, regardless of whether the country has happened to be a republic or monarchy. For centuries, members of the House of Orange maintained the effectively hereditary position of Stadtholder, the head of state, in the early modern Dutch Republic, and continued to do so until the state was absorbed into France's sphere of influence: first as the Batavian Republic and then into the expansionist French Empire of Emperor Napoleon I of the French. When the independence of the Dutch was restored after Napoleon's defeat, the Great Powers of Europe orchestrated the new United Kingdom of the Netherlands so that the House of Orange would now be guaranteed the position of head of state, except now as kings rather than Stadtholders. Though first Belgium then Luxembourg would secede from the Dutch Kingdom, the remaining Kingdom of the Netherlands continues to this day under the House of Orange, with the colour orange emerging as part of Dutch national identity as a result.

King William I of the United Kingdom of the Netherlands	1815–1839
King William I of the Kingdom of the Netherlands	1839–1840
King William II	1840–1849
King William III	1849–1890
Queen Wilhelmina	1890–1948
Queen Juliana	1948–1980
Queen Beatrix	1980–2013
King Willem-Alexander	2013–

House of Orleans

The House of Orleans has long been established, with the Dukes of Orleans leading the junior branch of the French royal family from the early modern era into modern times. With a revolutionary streak, the House of Orleans has taken several very controversial steps in relation to the historically more senior branch of the French royal family, the Bourbons, including providing active support for the revolutionary First French Republic, and even voting for the execution of their family member, the former King Louis XVI of France. Then, in the nineteenth century, the House of Orleans lingered in the background during the restoration of the Bourbons in France until the 1830 revolution, when Louis Philippe of Orleans emerged as King of the French, and so he remained for 18 years. He would be the last French king, despite the prospect of the House of Orleans retaking the French throne later in the nineteenth century, as part of the deal discussed with Henri, Count of Chambord, the Bourbon pretender to the throne. Since this high point, the Orleanists have been reduced to a minority movement, hoping to be restored as Kings of the French with seemingly little popular backing. In addition to contesting the French throne, the House of Orleans also gained an interest in the defunct throne of the Brazilian Empire: though this Empire was dissolved in the late nineteenth century, a hybrid dynasty, bringing the French House of Orleans and the Portuguese and Brazilian House of Braganza together, inherited the claim to the former Brazilian Imperial throne as a consequence of the marriage of an Orleanist prince to a daughter of the last Brazilian Emperor.

King Louis Philippe of the French 1830–1848

SECOND FRENCH REPUBLIC

Louis Philippe	1848–1850
Philippe VII	1850–1894
Philippe VIII	1894–1926
Jean III	1926–1940
Henri VI	1940–1999
Henri VII	1999–2019
Jean IV	2019–

House of Petrovic-Njegos

The House of Petrovic-Njegos has played an influential role in Montenegro for centuries: firstly as Prince-Bishops in the early modern period, then as Princes in the modern era, albeit formally playing a subordinate role to the Sultans of the House of Osman that ruled the Ottoman Empire. During the reign of Nikola Montenegro underwent drastic change, becoming independent as a principality which then became a kingdom on Nikola's golden jubilee. Although King Nikola was deposed, and his realm erased, with the creation of the Kingdom of Serbs, Croats and Slovenes after the First World War, his descendants have continued to remain high profile figures in Montenegro. King Nikola's grandson, Michael, had the opportunity to be installed as King of Montenegro during the Second World War, with the backing of the Axis Powers; while in turn Michael's son, Nikola, was not only invited to return to Montenegro by the Republic's government but was also provided with royal residences and a formal state function for himself and the House of Petrovic-Njegos, under a new law passed in 2011. This has made the prospective Nikola II the most influential member of the dynasty since his reigning namesake almost a century earlier, as well as the most influential royal in Eastern Europe since the fall of the monarchy in Greece in the 1970s.

Prince Nikola I of Montenegro	1878–1910
King Nikola I of Montenegro	1910–1918

KINGDOM OF SERBS, CROATS AND SLOVENES

Nikola I	1918–1921
Michael	1921–1986
Nikola II	1986–

House of Romanov

In the wake of instability and a power vacuum in early modern Russia, Michael Romanov was selected to become Tsar of Russia in 1613, being the first of his royal house to do so, with the Romanovs subsequently retaining the Russian throne for over 300 years. Though overseeing the expansion of their lands, which would form the largest contiguous country in the world, the Romanovs' grasp of the Russian throne would often be challenged, while they in turn would often resort to ruling their empire with an iron fist in an effort to retain it. Whilst the Romanovs would waver between autocracy and relative liberalism during their rule, at the turn of the twentieth century Tsar Nicholas II felt that the House of Romanov was at its most secure when it most strongly resisted concessions to democracy. This led to him stifling the efforts to reform Russia into some form of constitutional monarchy, which meant that Tsar Nicholas II, by concentrating power for himself, would primarily be associated with all of his country's successes, as well as failures. Russia's unsuccessful war effort, and general inability to maintain order and public confidence, during the First World War led to the two revolutions that first forced the Romanovs from the throne, and secondly made Russia into a communist state. Meanwhile, the new revolutionary government made their former Romanov rulers into their prisoners, and ultimately had them executed in 1918.

Empress Catherine II of Russia	1762–1796
Tsar Paul I	1796–1801
Tsar Alexander I	1801–1825
Tsar Nicholas I	1825–1855
Tsar Alexander II	1855–1881
Tsar Alexander III	1881–1894
Tsar Nicholas II	1894–1917

PROVISIONAL GOVERNMENT

Nicholas II	1917–1918
Cyril	1924–1938
Vladimir	1938–1992
Maria	1992–

House of Savoy

Originating from the Savoy region, covering parts of present-day France, Switzerland and Italy, the Savoy dynasty would come to prominence in the Italian peninsula, inheriting the throne of the Kingdom of Piedmont-Sardinia. Such was the potential of this state that it came to lead the movement for Italian unification from the middle of the nineteenth century, resulting in King Victor Emmanuel II of Piedmont-Sardinia becoming King of Italy. Just as the process of Italian unification seemed to come to an end, the House of Savoy looked to expand its reach further to the west as Prince Amadeo, the second son of King Victor Emmanuel II, was invited to become King of Spain in 1870, after Spain's Bourbon Queen Isabella II was deposed. However, King Amadeo's reign proved to be short and difficult, abdicating after just a few years on the throne and declaring Spain 'ungovernable'. During the Second World War, encouraged by the ambitions of the Italian dictator Benito Mussolini, to the east now the House of Savoy was set to make the Balkans its own sphere of influence, with close relatives of the Italian royal family to rule Croatia and Montenegro, while King Victor Emmanuel III of Italy became King of Albania as well. Ultimately, defeat in the War ended the House of Savoy's ambitions not only in the Balkans, but also led to a referendum that forced the abdication of King Umberto II of Italy after just one month on the throne, hence why he became known as 'the May King'.

King Victor Emmanuel III of the Albanians (King Victor Emmanuel III of Italy) 1939–1943

PEOPLE'S SOCIALIST REPUBLIC OF ALBANIA

KINGDOM OF PIEDMONT-SARDINIA and other Italian states

King Victor Emmanuel II of Italy	1861–1878
King Umberto I	1878–1900
King Victor Emmanuel III	1900–1946
King Umberto II	1946

ITALIAN REPUBLIC

Umberto II	1946–1983
Victor Emmanuel IV	1983–

PROVISIONAL GOVERNMENT

King Amadeo of Spain   1870–1873

FIRST SPANISH REPUBLIC

House of Saxe-Coburg-Gotha

Despite starting out as the rulers of a small German duchy of the same name, the dynasty of Saxe-Coburg-Gotha would punch well above its weight in the nineteenth century. Members of this royal house would come to rule in the furthest corners of Europe: Bulgaria to the southeast, Portugal to the southwest, and Great Britain and Belgium in the northwest. Their influence would reach further still thanks to the overseas empires of these European nations. However, these remarkable gains would promptly be reversed in the first half of the twentieth century: Portugal's republican revolution in 1910 toppled the monarchy, with the Portuguese branch of the dynasty becoming extinct with the death of King Manuel II, the last Portuguese monarch. Within the subsequent decade this German royal house, which Queen Victoria of Great Britain had been so proud to see succeed her due to its association with her beloved Prince Albert, became an embarrassment during the First World War, as Germany was the foremost enemy of both Great Britain and Belgium, prompting Queen Victoria's grandson, King George V, to change the name of Britain's reigning dynasty to the House of Windsor, and sever his family's numerous ties with Germany. The downfall of the monarchy in Germany also brought about the end of the royal house's dynastic home, as the Duchy of Saxe-Coburg-Gotha was dissolved at the end of the First World War. Then, the Saxe-Coburg-Gothas lost Bulgaria as the young Tsar Simeon II was ousted by the communist government that was installed there shortly after the Second World War.

UNITED KINGDOM OF THE NETHERLANDS

King Leopold I of the Belgians	1831–1865
King Leopold II	1865–1909
King Albert I	1909–1934
King Leopold III	1934–1951
King Baudouin	1951–1993
King Albert II	1992–2013
King Philippe	2013–

HOUSE OF HANOVER

King Edward VII of Great Britain and Ireland	1901–1910
King George V	1910–1917

HOUSE OF WINDSOR

House of Windsor

Although this is the British branch of the House of Saxe-Coburg-Gotha, the embarrassment for the British royal family during the First World War of their overwhelmingly strong ties with Germany was encapsulated by the name of its reigning royal house. Concerned that the hardships of war, and the capricious mood of the public, could inspire the British to turn against their seemingly Germanic monarchs during the darkest days of the War, it was decided that a name change was best for the British royal family. After considering various contenders, and whether to revert to an old British name or to fabricate a completely new one, it was decided that King George V should be the first monarch of the new House of Windsor, named after his favoured royal residence, Windsor Castle. Despite significant change since, overseeing ups and downs for Great Britain and her monarchy alike, the House of Windsor has now endured for over a century.

HOUSE OF SAXE-COBURG-GOTHA

King George V of Great Britain and Ireland	1917–1921
King George V of Great Britain and Northern Ireland	1921–1936
King Edward VIII	1936
King George VI	1936–1952
Queen Elizabeth II	1952–

House of Wittelsbach

A German dynasty, the House of Wittelsbach reigned in Bavaria for centuries, emerging as Kings of Bavaria in the nineteenth century. The Wittelsbachs would for a long time play a subordinate role, as Bavarian rulers ranked beneath the Habsburgs during the early modern era as part of the Holy Roman Empire, then later when the Kings of Bavaria held a junior position under the Hohenzollern dynasty in the German Empire. However, Bavaria consistently maintained at least a degree of self-government, and the Wittelsbach dynasty had the chance to rule their own new and independent Kingdom of Greece, with Otto, son of King Ludwig I of Bavaria, appointed to establish the Greek monarchy in 1832. However, though King Otto's Greece endured for several decades, the relationship between King and country often appeared to be a difficult one, with King Otto ultimately forced from the throne in 1862, and replaced as King by a prince of the House of Glucksburg. Thereafter the House of Wittelsbach gave up on the Greek throne, but continued to be a significant European royal house: firstly because of the Kingdom of Bavaria, though this was dissolved at the end of the First World War, along with the other monarchies of the German Empire; but also thanks to their long pedigree, meaning the Wittelsbachs tended to be popular choices for royal marriages. This has continued even to recent times, with Sophie, born a titular Duchess of Bavaria, likely to become a prominent member of the Wittelsbach dynasty in the present day thanks to her marriage to Prince Alois, current heir to the Principality of Liechtenstein.

OTTOMAN EMPIRE

King Otto I of Greece   1832–1862

HOUSE OF GLUCKSBURG

House of Zogu

Though only established as a royal house in 1928 when Ahmet Zogu, hitherto President of Albania, declared himself King of the Albanians, the new King Zog I nevertheless claimed to be descended from King Skanderbeg, monarch of the medieval Kingdom of Albania. Though King Zog, and his Zogu dynasty, would only retain the Albanian throne for 11 years, by which time the House of Zogu was deposed by invading Italian armies, the former King Zog and his descendants would continue to claim the Albanian crown, achieving varying degrees of success and popularity, but never quite reaching the point of restoration.

ALBANIAN REPUBLIC

King Zog I of the Albanians   1928–1939

HOUSE OF SAVOY

Zog I   1939–1961
Leka I   1961–2011
Leka II   2011–

Appendix II

Royal Intermarriage, Queen Victoria Of Great Britain, Her Children and Grandchildren, And Their Consorts

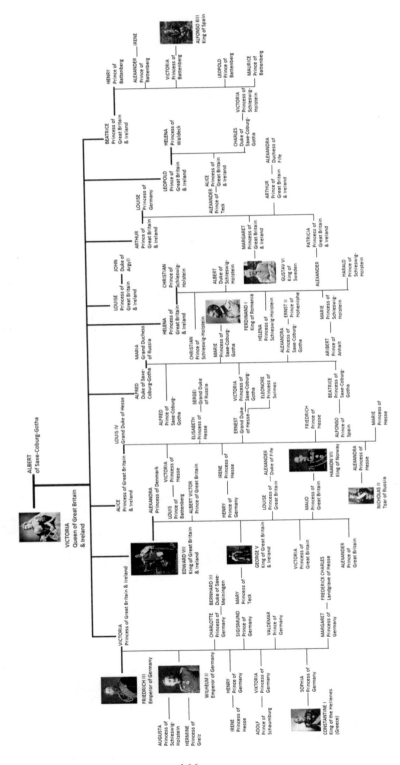

Bibliography

Text

Books

Abrams, Lynn. 'Bismarck and the German Empire: 1871–1918', 2007

Aldous, Richard. 'The Lion and the Unicorn', 2006

Belien, Paul. 'A Throne in Brussels: Britain, the Saxe-Coburgs and the Belgianisation of Europe', 2014

Brook-Shepherd, Gordon. 'The Last Habsburg', 1968

Brook-Shepherd, Gordon. 'Uncrowned Emperor: The Life and Times of Otto von Habsburg', 2007

Byers, Ann. 'Rescuing the Danish Jews: A Heroic Story from the Holocaust', 2012

Cadbury, Deborah. 'Queen Victoria's Matchmaking', 2017

Cannadine, David. 'George V: The Unexpected King', 2014

Clegg, Richard. 'A Concise History of Greece', 2002

Cline, Teresa. 'Single White Female Backpacker', 2012

Danstrup, John. 'A History of Denmark', 1948

de Bernardy, Francoise. 'Princes of Monaco: The Remarkable History of the Grimaldi Family', 1961

de Vilallonga; Jose Luis. 'The King: A Life of King Juan Carlos of Spain', 1994

Devere-Summers, Anthony. 'War and the Royal Houses of Europe in the Twentieth Century', 1996

Edwards, Anne. 'The Grimaldis of Monaco: Centuries of Scandal, Years of Grace', 2017

Eliot, Alexander. 'Greece: A History', 2016

Everdell, William R. 'The End of Kings: A History of Republics and Republicans', 2000

Fenby, Jonathan. 'The History of Modern France', 2015

Ferguson, Niall. 'The War of the World: History's Age of Hatred', 2006

Fleming, Ian. 'The Man with the Golden Gun', 1965

Griffiths, Katie. 'The Spanish Civil War', 2017

Hall, Richard C. 'Consumed by War: European Conflict in the 20th Century', 2015

Halsey, Francis W. 'The Literary Digest History of the World War Vol. X', 1919

Hanbury-Tenison, Robin. 'Land of Eagles: Riding Through Europe's Forgotten Country', 2014

Hauge, Kari. 'Famous Family Trees', 2018

Heaton-Armstrong, Duncan. 'The Six Month Kingdom: Albania1914', 2005

Jesperson, J.V. Knud. 'A History of Denmark', 2011

Kaika, Maria and Karaliotas, Lazaros. 'Athens' Syntagma Square Reloaded: From Staging Disagreement Towards Instituting Democratic Spaces' in Hou, Jeffrey and Knierbein, Sabine. 'City Unsilenced: Urban Resistance and Public Space in the Age of Shrinking Democracy', 2017

Katritzki, Freda. 'The World of Private Castles, Palaces and Estates', 2005

Koliopoulos, John S. and Veremis, Thanos M. 'Modern Greece: A History since 1821', 2009

Kostis, Kostas. 'History's Spoiled Children: The Formation of the Modern Greek State', 2018

Louda, Jiri and Maclagan, Michael. 'Lines of Succession: Heraldry of the Royal Families of Europe', 1981

Lowe, Norman. 'Mastering Modern World History', 2005

Mak, Geert. 'In Europe: Travels through the twentieth century', 2008

Marr, Andrew. 'The Diamond Queen', 2011

Martin, Frederick. 'The Statesman's Yearbook: statistical and historical annual of the states of the civilised world handbook for politicians and merchants for the year 1872', 1872

Martin, George RR. 'A Game of Thrones', 2011

McMurty Longo, James. 'Isabel Orleans-Braganca: The Brazilian Princess Who Freed the Slaves', 2007

Merriman, John. 'A History of Modern Europe: Volume Two: From the French Revolution to the Present', 2010

Montgomery-Massingberd, Hugh. 'Burke's Royal Families of the World', 1977

Murphy, Paul Thomas. 'Shooting Victoria: Madness, Mayhem, and the Rebirth of the British Monarchy', 2012

Nielsen, Christian Axboe. 'Making Yugoslavs: Identity in King Aleksandar's Yugoslavia', 2014

Opfell, Olga S. 'Royalty Who Wait: The 21 Heads of Formerly Regnant Houses of Europe', 2001

Palmer, Alan. 'Bernadotte', 1990

Palmer, Alan. 'Twilight of the Habsburgs: The Life and Times of Emperor Francis Joseph', 2014

Paxman, Jeremy. 'On Royalty', 2007

Radzinsky, Edvard. 'Alexander II: The Last Great Tsar', 2005

Ralph Lewis, Brenda. 'The Untold History of the Kings and Queens of Europe', 2016

Ridley, Jane. 'Victoria: Queen, Matriarch, Empress', 2015

Röhl, John C. G. 'Kaiser Wilhelm II: A Concise Life', 2014

Snyder, Timothy. 'The Red Prince: The Fall of a Dynasty and the Rise of Modern Europe', 2009

Starkey, David. 'Crown & Country: The Kings and Queens of England', 2010

Strauss-Schom, Alan. 'The Shadow Emperor', 2018

Tomasevich, Jozo. 'War and Revolution in Yugoslavia: 1941–1945', 2002

Thomson, David. 'Europe since Napoleon', 1966

Ulwencreutz, Lars. 'Ulwencreutz's The Royal Families in Europe V', 2013von Rauch, Georg. 'The Baltic States: The years of independence, Estonia, Latvia and Lithuania 1917–1940', 1995

Wagar, Chip. 'Double Emperor: The Life and Times of Francis of Austria', 2018

Wielenga, Friso. 'A History of the Netherlands: from the Sixteenth Century to the Present Day', 2015

Wilson, Keith M. 'The International Impact of the Boer War', 2014

Witte, Els, Craeybeckx, Jan and Meynen, Alain. 'Political History of Belgium: From 1830 Onwards', 2009

Wortman, Richard. 'Scenarios of Power: From Alexander II to the abdication of Nicholas II', 1995

Websites

albanianroyalcourt.al
almanachdegotha.org
Balkaninsight.com
Bbc.co.uk
Britannica.com
Comtedeparis.com
Express.co.uk
Fuerstenhaus.li
Imperialhouse.ru
Irishtimes.com
La-couronne.org
Montecarlosbm.com
Royal.uk
Royalfamily.org
Telegraph.co.uk
Thecommonwealth.org
Theguardian.com
Web.archive.org

Images

Coats of arms: en.wikipedia.org, checked against Jiri Louda and Michael Maclagan's book 'Line of Succession: Heraldry of the Royal Families of Europe', and the websites albanianroyalcourt.al and windsor-berkshire.co.uk.

Gallery: en.wikipedia.org, checked against Britannica.com, almanachdegotha.org and aforementioned books.

Flags: en.wikipedia.org

Family Tree: Pictures from en.wikipedia.org, checked against Deborah Cadbury's book 'Queen Victoria's Matchmaking' and Britannica.com